SELECTED SAYINGS OF

THE HOLY PROPHET OF ISLAM

(Arabic text with English Translation)

Selected Sayings of
The Holy Prophet of Islam^{sa}
(Arabic text with English Translation)

First published in UK in 1988
Reprinted in different countries several times.

Editions Published in Qadian, India in 2012, 2013, 2015 .
Present Edition printed in Qadian, India in March 2016.

Copies: 6000

© Islam International Publications Ltd.

Published By:
Nazarat Nashr-o-Isha'at,
Sadr Anjuman Ahmadiyya Qadian,
Distt: Gurdaspur, Punjab-143516 (INDIA)

Printed in INDIA at Fazle Umar Printing Press Qadian.

ISBN: 978-81-7912-353-9

In celebration of the Centenary of the Worldwide Ahmadiyya Community.

This is a gift from those Ahmadi Muslims who, even in this age, are being persecuted and martyred merely because they love and proclaim the Unity of God. They are an embodiment of the spirit of Bilal.*

*Bilal (may God be pleased with him) was one of the companions of the Holy Prophet Muhammad, peace be upon him. Though he was subjected to extreme forms of torture due to his conversion to Islam, he was prepared to die rather than renounce his belief in the Unity of God.

CONTENTS

PREFACE

Islam is a great religion. The secret of its greatness lies in the complete and perfect teachings of the Holy Qur'an and in the fact that the Founder of Islam, the Holy Prophet Muhammad peace and blessings of Allah be upon him, practiced these teachings to the fullest extent. He thus became a perfect and living example of what he taught.

The deep and unbreakable relationship between his practice and teachings left an idelible impression on his Companions. After his death, when his wife Ayesha was asked about the life of the Holy Prophet Muhammad , peace and blessings of Allah be upon him, her answer was:

كَانَ خُلُقُهُ الْقُرْآن

"His life was the Qur'an ".

There was no contradiction between his word and the Word of God. His revelation was pure, without the least reflection of his personal desires. The Holy Qur'an bears this testimony about him:

وَمَايَنْطِقُ عَنِ الْهَوٰى اِنْ هُوَاِلَّا وَحْيٌ يُوْحىٰ

"He does not say anything from his own self; all his sayings are in accordance with Divine revelation."

(CH. 53: Al-Najm 4-5)

No wonder then that he is presented in the Holy Qur'an as a perfect model for the whole of mankind and for all times to come. God Almighty says in the Holy Qur'an:

لَكُم فِيْ رَسُوْلِ اللّٰهِ أُسْوَةٌ حَسَنَةٌ

"For you there is a noble example in the Prophet of God."

(CH. 33 Al-Ahzab: 22)

Here, a short selection of *Ahadith*, that is, Traditions regarding the life, actions and sayings of the Holy Prophet, peace and blessings of Allah be upon him, is presented. A study of these sayings provides a brief introduction to the everyday life of the Holy Prophet, peace and blessings of Allah be upon him, as well as to his prayers, high moral standards, and his style of preaching.

Though some Traditions are reported to have been written during the lifetime of the Holy Prophet, peace and blessings of Allah be upon him, most of them were committed to writing some 200 years after his demise. Despite the fact that most Traditions were collected after such a long period, they can still be considered highly reliable in the light of the following:

As the words of the Holy Prophet, peace and blessings of Allah be upon him, were held in very high esteem, all of what he said was immediately memorized by his companions and subsequently repeated, reported and talked about among themselves innumerable times.

The second important factor is that his words were treated with great religious fervour and devotion. Any interpolation or even slight deviation from his original words was considered a crime for which one was answerable to God. The words used by the Holy Prophet, peace and blessings of Allah be upon him, himself were,

"Hell would be the abode of a person who
attributes to me that which I did not say."

Thirdly, when people related things about him or from him to others, it was a custom for the receiver of such a message, not only to memorize what he was told, but also to commit to memory the name and particulars of the person who related it to him, so that if his word was questioned, he could quote the authority.

The fourth important aspect is that the Arabs were famous for their excellent memory, ant that even before the advent of the Holy Prophet, peace and blessings of Allah be upon him, it was not rare to find among them people who had memorized 100,000 verses of Arab poets or even more. In addition to this, it was a common custom to remember family trees. After the advent of the Holy Prophet, peace and blessings of Allah be upon him, the moral standard of his followers was raised to a very high degree, and the habit of exaggeration was particularly condemned. Furthermore, great emphasis was laid in the Holy Qur'an, not only on truth, but also on the verification of statements.

As a result of these factors, the Traditions of the Holy Prophet of Islam, peace and blessings of Allah be upon him, were treated with very special care, unknown to other systems of collection of historical material.

In the process of collecting these sayings, Muslim scholars worked so meticulously and so much attention was given to accuracy, that the collection of no other historical data can be compared with the compilation of the sayings of the Holy Prophet of Islam, peace and blessings of Allah be upon him. Every link in the chain of narrators of a particular Tradition is specified in the major works of Hadith. Even the study of the character of the narrators and their reliablity developed into a field of research in its own right. As a result, a new form of knowledge concerning the analysis of Traditions came into being for the first time in human history.

For the benefit of those readers who know very little about Islam, we must mention here that out of the scores of books written on the subject of the Traditions, six are considered to be of extraordinary importance by Muslim scholars. They are known as the *Sihah Sittah* (The Six Authentic Ones). Most of the Traditions presented in this short collection are taken from these six books. The following is a brief introduction to these books and to the scholars responsible for their compilation:

SAHIH BUKHARI:

This book is considered to be the most authentic book after the Holy Qur'an. The compiler thereof is Muhammad Ismail of Bukhara, commonly known as Imam Bukhari.

(b. 194, d. 256 Hijra; 816-878 A.D.)

SAHIH MUSLIM:

Considered second in importance is Sahih Muslim. This was compiled by Muslim bin Al Hajjaj who was a native of Neshapur in Khorasan. (b. 202, d.261 Hijra; 824- 883 A.D.)

JAMI AL TIRMIDHI:

Third in order is Jami Al Tirmidhi. The compiler, Imam Muhammad bin Isa was a native of Tirmidh.

(b. 209, d. 279 Hijra; 831-901 A.D.)

SUNAN ABU DAUD:

Next is Sunan Abu Daud, compiled by Sulaiman bin Al Ashah, known as Abu Daud. (b. 202, d. 275 Hijra; 824-897 A.D.)

SUNAN IBN MAJAH:

Considered fifth in degree of authenticity is Sunan ibn Majah. It was compiled by Muhammad bin Majah who was from the famous city of Qizwin in Iraq. (b. 209, d.275 Hijra; 831-897 A.D.)

SUNAN NISAI:

The sixth book is Sunan Nisai. It was compiled by Ahmad bin Shuaib, known as "Nisai" after the city of Nisa in Khorasan.

(b. 215, d. 306 Hijra; 837-928 A.D.)

MUWATTA IMAM MALIK:

Besides the Sihah Sittah (The Six Authentic Ones), there is another very important compilation of Traditions known as Muwatta Imam Malik. The compiler, Malik bin Anas, is commonly known as Imam Malik. This book is not included among the Sihah Sittah as it is primarily considered to be a book of jurisprudence, and the Traditions are quoted mostly in discussions of juristic issues. The authenticity of the narrations quoted in Muwatta Imam Malik can be judged by the fact that all of them are included in Sahih Bukhari and Sahih Muslim. Imam Malik's status among the compilers of Traditions is so high that he is known as 'Imamul Muhaddithin' (the leader of the compilers), and all of them have borne testimony to his exalted position.

This selection from the sayings of the Holy Prophet of Islam, peace and blessings of Allah be upon him, was made by Hadhrat Mirza Tahir Ahmad, Khalifatul Masih IV, the Supreme Head of the Worldwide Ahmadiyya Muslim Community from 1982 to 2003.

This selection covers the following important subjects.:-

1 Intentions and Actions
2 The Majesty of the Lord of Honour
3 The Love of the Lord   4 The Holy Qur'an
5 The Excellent Conduct of the Messenger of Allah
6 The Foundations of Islam   7 Fasting
8 The Hajj   9 The Zakaat
10 Enjoining Good and Forbidding Evil
11 Inviting People to Allah
12 Obligations and Prohibitions   13 Marriage
14 Good Conduct   15 The Islamic Society
16 Being Grateful to People
17 The Good Treatment of Parents   18 Good Neighbourliness
19 Kindness   20 Forgiveness
21 Table Manners   22 Matters of Dress
23 Cleanliness   24 Envy
25 Arrogance   26 The Decline of Islam
27 The Advent of Imam Mahdi

This selection from the sayings of the Holy Prophet of Islam, peace and blessings of Allah be upon him, was a part of the program commemorating the Centenary Celebrations of the

Ahmadiyya Muslim Jama'at. It was translated into many different languages and widely spread in the world. Any queries regarding the availability of its translations in various languages should be directed to the publishers or to any Ahmadiyya Muslim Mission in any country of the world or visit www.alislam.org for more information.

We hope and pray that while this attempt will succeed in quenching some of the thirst for knowledge it will also generate a craving for learning more.

Naseer Ahmad Qamar
Additional Wakil-ul- Isha'at London
November 2011

Intentions and Actions

١ـ حَدَّثَنَا الْحُمَيْدِيُّ قَالَ حَدَّثَنَا سُفْيَانُ قَالَ حَدَّثَنَا يَحْيَ بْنُ
سَعِيْدٍالْأَنْصَارِيُّ قَالَ أَخْبَرَنِيْ مُحَمَّدُ بْنُ إِبْرَاهِيْمَ التَّيْمِيُّ أَنَّهُ
سَمِعَ عَلْقَمَةَ بْنَ وَقَّاصٍ اللَّيْثِيَّ يَقُوْلُ سَمِعْتُ عُمَرَبْنَ
الْخَطَّابِ رضى الله عنه عَلَى الْمِنْبَرِ قَالَ سَمِعْتُ رَسُوْلَ اللهِ
ﷺ يَقُوْلُ : اِنَّمَا الْأَعْمَالُ بِالنِّيَّاتِ وَاِنَّمَا لِكُلِّ امْرِئٍ مَّانَوَى ،
فَمَنْ كَانَتْ هِجْرَتُهُ اِلَى اللهِ وَ رَسُوْلِهِ فَهِجْرَتُهُ اِلَى اللهِ وَ
رَسُوْلِهِ وَمَنْ كَانَتْ هِجْرَتُهُ لِدُنْيَا يُصِيْبُهَا ، أَوِامْرَأَةٍ يَنْكِحُهَا
فَهِجْرَتُهُ اِلَى مَا هَاجَرَاِلَيْهِ ـ

« بخارى باب كيف كان بدء الوحى الى رسول الله ﷺ »

1. Umar, God be pleased with him, narrates the following while he was addressing from the pulpit: "I heard the Holy Prophet, peace and blessings of Allah be upon him, saying the following: 'Deeds are determined by intentions alone. Man will only get that which he really intends. The migration of the one who truly intends to migrate towards Allah and His Messenger will lead him to Allah and His messenger. But whoever keeps worldly objects in view will only get worldly objects. If a man migrates intending to marry a woman that will be his reward. *(Bukhari)*

٢ ـ عَنْ عَبْدِ اللهِ بْنِ عَمْرٍو بْنِ الْعَاصِ رضى الله عنه عَنِ النَّبِيِّ
ﷺ قَالَ : الْمُسْلِمُ مَنْ سَلِمَ الْمُسْلِمُوْنَ مِنْ لِسَانِهِ وَ يَدِهِ
وَالْمُهَاجِرُ مَنْ هَجَرَ مَانَهَى اللهُ عَنْهُ ـ « بخارى كتاب الايمان
باب المسلم من سلم . . . . »

2. Abdullah bin 'Amr, God be pleased with him, states that he heard the Holy Prophet, peace and blessings of Allah be upon him, say: "The true Muslim is he from whose hands and from whose tongue other Muslims are safe. The true emigrant is he who forsakes that which is forbidden by God." *(Bukhari)*

The Majesty of the Lord of Honour

٣- عَنْ عَبْدِ اللهِ بْنِ عُمَرَ رضى الله تعالى عنهما قَالَ قَرَأَ رَسُوْلُ اللهِ ﷺ هذِهِ الْاٰيَةَ وَهُوَ عَلَى الْمِنْبَرِ: وَالسَّمٰوٰتُ مَطْوِيَّاتٌ بِيَمِيْنِهِ ، سُبْحَانَهُ وَتَعَالٰى عَمَّا يُشْرِكُوْنَ ، قَالَ يَقُوْلُ اللهُ اَنَاالْجَبَّارُ ، اَنَا الْمُتَكَبِّرُ ، اَنَا الْمَلِكُ ، اَنَا الْمُتَعَالُ يُمَجِّدُ نَفْسَهُ قَالَ فَجَعَلَ رَسُوْلُ اللهِ ﷺ يُرَدِّدُهَا ، حَتّٰى رَجَفَ بِهَاالْمِنْبَرُ حَتّٰى ظَنَنَّا اَنَّهُ سَيَخِرُّ بِهِ ـ

« مسند احمد ص ٨٨/ ٢ »

3.   Abdullah bin Umar, God be pleased with him, narrates that the Holy Prophet, peace and blessings of Allah be upon him, stated, while delivering a Friday Sermon from the pulpit:

"The heavens are rolled up in His right hand. Holy is He and far exalted above the idolatry in which they indulge." The Holy Prophet, peace and blessings of Allah be upon him, further stated that Allah The Almighty says, 'I am the One Who has complete power to reform, conscious of My Greatness, The Sovereign, The Lofty." The Holy Prophet, peace and blessings of Allah be upon him, kept repeating these words with such force that the pulpit started shaking and we were concerned lest it should collapse under him." *(Musnad Ahmad)*

٤ ـ عَنْ اَبِىْ هُرَيْرَةَ رضى الله عنه قَالَ : قَالَ النَّبِىُّ ﷺ كَلِمَتَانِ
حَبِيْبَتَـانِ اِلَى الـرَّحْمَـانِ خَفِيْفَتَـانِ عَلَى اللِّسَانِ ثَقِيْلَتَانِ فِى
الْمِيْزَانِ : سُبْحَانَ اللهِ وَ بِحَمْدِهِ سُبْحَانَ اللهِ الْعَظِيْمِ ـ

« بخارى كتاب الرد على الجهنية . . . باب قول الله يضع
الموازين بالقسط »

4. Abu Hurairah, God be pleased with him, narrates that the
Holy Prophet, peace and blessings of Allah be upon him, said:

"There are two expressions which are very dear to God The
Beneficent. They are light on the tongue but are immensely
weighty in substance, and they are:
(Subhan Allah wa bi Hamdihi; Subhan Allahil Azim)
"Exalted is Allah with all His Glory; Exalted is Allah with all
His Majesty." *(Bukhari)*

٥ ـ عَنْ هَمَّامِ بْنِ مُنَبِّهٍ قَالَ هٰذَامَا حَدَّثَنَـابِهِ اَبُوْهُرَيْرَةَ عَنْ
رَسُوْلِ اللهِ ﷺ قَالَ اللهُ عَزَّوَجَلَّ كَذَّبَنِىْ عَبْدِىْ ، وَلَمْ يَكُنْ
لَهُ ذٰلِكَ ، وَشَتَمَنِىْ وَلَمْ يَكُنْ لَهُ ذٰلِكَ تَكْذِيْبُهُ اِيَّاىَ ، اَنْ
يَقُوْلَ لَنْ يُعِيْدَنَا كَمَا بَدَأَنَا ، وَاَمَّا شَتَمَهُ اِيَّاىَ يَقُوْلُ اِتَّخَذَ اللهُ
وَلَدًا ، وَاَنَا الصَّمَدُ الَّذِىْ لَمْ اَلِدْ ، وَ لَمْ اُوْلَدْ ، وَلَمْ يَكُنْ لِّىْ
كُفُوًا اَحَدٌ ـ

« مسند احمد ص ٣١٧/٢ »

5. Abu Hurairah, God be pleased with him, narrates that the
Holy Prophet, peace and blessings of Allah be upon him,
mentioned that Allah The Almighty states:

"My servant transgresses against Me, while it does not behove him to do so. He abuses Me, while it does not behove him to do so. His transgression against Me is that he says that 'Allah the Almighty, having once created me, will not resurrect me (after I am dead).' And his abuse of Me is that he claims that 'Allah has taken unto Himself a son,' whereas I am Self Sufficient, The One on Whom everything else depends. 1 have never begot, nor was I begotten, and there never was one like unto Me."

(Musnad Ahmad)

٦ ـ عَنْ جَابِـرٍ رضى الله عنـه قَالَ: سَمِعْتُ رَسُوْلَ الله ﷺ يَقُوْلُ: اَفْضَلُ الذِّكْرِ لَا اِلهَ اِلَّا اللهُ وَاَفْضَلُ الدُّعَاءِ اَلْحَمْدُلله ـ

« ترمذى كتاب الدعوات دعوة المسلم مستجابة »

6. Jabir, God be pleased with him, narrates that he heard the Holy Prophet, peace and blessings of Allah be upon him, state:

"The most excellent way of remembering Allah is to proclaim: There is no one worthy of worship except Allah. And the best supplication is to profess: All praise belongs to Allah." *(Tirmidhi)*

٧ ـ عَنْ اَبِىْ مُوْسَى الاَشْعَـرِىِّ رضى الله عنه عَنِ النَّبِىِّ ﷺ قَالَ: مَثَـلُ الَـذِىْ يَذْكُـرُ رَبَّهُ وَالَذِىْ لَايَذْكُرُهُ مَثَلُ الْحَىِّ وَالْمَيِّتِ وَرَوَاهُ مُسْلِمٌ فَقَالَ: مَثَلُ الْبَيْتِ الَّذِىْ يُذْكَرُ اللهُ فِيْهِ وَالْبَيْتِ الَّذِىْ لَايُذْكَرُ اللهُ فِيْهِ مَثَلُ الْحَىِّ وَالْمَيِّتِ ٭

« بخارى كتاب الدعوات باب فضل ذكر الله تعالى »

7. Abu Musa al Ash'ari, God be pleased with him, narrates that the Holy Prophet, peace and blessings of Allah be upon him, stated:

"The case of the one who remembers Allah as against the one

who does not, is like that of the living as compared to the dead. The case of the house in which Allah is remembered and the one in which He is not remembered, is like that of the living as compared to the dead." *(Bukhari)*

٨ ـ عَنْ اَبِىْ مُوْسٰى قَالَ كُنَّامَعَ النَّبِىِّ ﷺ فِىْ سَفَرٍ فَجَعَلَ النَّاسُ يَجْهَرُوْنَ بِالتَّكْبِيْرِ فَقَالَ النَّبِىُّ ﷺ اَيُّهَا النَّاسُ اِرْبَعُوْ عَلَى اَنْفُسِكُمْ اِنَّكُمْ لَيْسَ تَدْعُوْنَ اَصَمَّ وَلَا غَائِبًا اِنَّكُمْ تَدْعُوْنَ سَمِيْعًا قَرِيْبًا وَهُوَمَعَكُمْ ـ

« مسلم كتاب الذكر استحباب خفض الصوت بالذكر »

8. Abu Musa, God be pleased with him, narrates:

"Once while we were on a journey with the Holy Prophet, peace and blessings of Allah be upon him, people started exclaiming rather loudly, *'Allahu Akbar*!' (God is the Greatest). The Holy Prophet, peace and blessings of Allah be upon him, said:

O' people! Adopt a course of moderation. You are not addressing one who is deaf or absent. You are addressing The One Who is All Hearing, Ever Present and is already with you.'

(Muslim)

٩ ـ عَنْ اَبِىْ هُرَيْرَةَ عَنِ النَّبِىِّ ﷺ قَالَ : اِنَّ لِلّٰهِ تَبَارَكَ وَ تَعَالٰى مَلَائِكَةً سَيَّارَةً فُضْلًا يَتْبَعُوْنَ مَجَالِسَ الذِّكْرِ فَاِذَا وَجَدُوْا مَجْلِسًا فِيْهِ ذِكْرٌ قَعَدُوْامَعَهُمْ وَحَفَّ بَعْضُهُمْ بَعْضًا بِاَجْنِحَتِهِمْ حَتّٰى يَمْلَؤُا مَابَيْنَهُمْ وَبَيْنَ السَّمَآءِ الدُّنْيَا فَاِذَا تَفَرَّقُوْا عَرَجُوْا وَصَعِدُوْا اِلَى السَّمَآءِ ۔ قَالَ فَيَسْاَلُهُمُ اللّٰهُ عَزَّوَجَلَّ وَهُوَ اَعْلَمُ بِهِمْ مِنْ اَيْنَ جِئْتُمْ ؟ فَيَقُوْلُوْنَ جِئْنَامِنْ عِنْدِ عِبَادِكَ فِى اَلْاَرْضِ يُسَبِّحُوْنَكَ وَيُكَبِّرُوْنَكَ وَيُهَلِّلُوْنَكَ وَيَحْمِدُوْنَكَ وَيَسْئَلُوْنَكَ قَالَ وَمَاذَا يَسْاَلُوْنِىْ قَالُوْا يَسْئَلُوْنَكَ جَنَّتَكَ قَالَ وَهَلْ رَاَوْا جَنَّتِىْ قَالُوْا لَااَىْ رَبِّ ، قَالَ فَكَيْفَ لَوْ رَاَوْا جَنَّتِىْ

قَالُوْا وَيَسْتَجِيْرُوْنَكَ قَالَ وَمِمَّ يَسْتَجِيْرُوْنِيْ قَالُوْا مِنْ نَارِكَ
يَارَبِّ قَالَ وَهَلْ رَأَوْا نَارِىْ قَالُوْا لَا ، قَالَ فَكَيْفَ لَورَأَوْا
نَارِىْ ـ قَالَ وَيَسْتَغْفِـرُوْنَـكَ قَالَ فَيَقُوْلُ قَدْ غَفَرْتُ هُمْ
فَأَعْطَيْتُهُمْ مَاسَأَلُوْا وَأَجَرْتُهُمْ مِمَّا اسْتَجَارُوْا قَالَ فَيَقُوْلُوْنَ رَبِّ
فِيْهِمْ فُلَانٌ عَبْدٌ خَطَاءٌ اِنَّمَا مَرَّ فَجَلَسَ مَعَهُمْ قَالَ فَيَقُوْلُ وَلَهُ
غَفَرْتُ ، هُمُ الْقَوْمُ لَايَشْقَى بِهِمْ جَلِيْسُهُمْ ـ
« مسلم كتاب الذكر باب فضل مجالس الذكر »

9. Abu Hurairah, God be pleased with him, narrates that the Holy Prophet, peace and blessings of Allah be upon him, said:

To Allah belong some angels of high rank who are always on the move in search of people who assemble for the purpose of remembering Allah. When they come upon an assembly engaged in the remembrance of Allah The Almighty, the angels begin to join them, extending their wings over them, hovering one upon another until the space between the earth and the nearest heaven is filled with their presence. When people disperse, they too depart ascending back to heaven. Then The Almighty asks them, (while He knows full well what had happened), 'Where do you come from?' They answer, 'We come from some servants of Thine who were exalting Thee, extolling Thy greatness, proclaiming Thy Unity, glorifying Thee and supplicating Thee. 'Then The Almighty enquires, 'What did they beg of me?' The angels say, 'They were begging Thee for Thy paradise.' Then Allah enquires, 'Have they seen My paradise?' The angels reply, 'No, our Lord, they have not seen Thy paradise'. 'What if they had seen My paradise!' exclaims Allah. 'They also seek refuge in Thee,' continue the angels. Allah says, 'From what do they seek My refuge?' 'From Thy fire,' they reply. Allah asks, 'Have they seen My fire?' The angels reply, 'No, they have not.' 'What if they had seen My fire!' exclaims Allah. Then the angels say, 'They ask for Thy forgiveness.' Allah replies,

'That I have already granted them; also I have bestowed upon them all that they ever beseeched of Me, and I have given them the refuge that they sought of Me.' Then, the angels say, '0 our Lord, there was one among them who was extremely sinful. He was just passing by and chose to sit a while with them.' 'Even him I have forgiven,' says Allah. 'They are so blessed that no one who happens to be in their company remains unblessed."* *(Muslim)*

(* This is a figurative expression of the ever increasing blessings of God upon such an assembly and should not be taken too literally).

The Love of the Lord

١٠ - عَنْ أَبِى الدَّرْدَاءِ رضى الله عنه قَالَ : قَالَ رَسُوْلُ اللهِ ﷺ كَانَ
مِنْ دُعَاءِ دَاؤُدَ عَلَيْهِ السَّلَامُ : اَللّٰهُمَّ اِنِّىْ اَسْأَلُكَ حُبَّكَ وَحُبَّ
مَنْ يُحِبُّكَ وَالْعَمَلَ الَّذِىْ يُبَلِّغُنِىْ حُبَّكَ ، اللّٰهُمَّ اجْعَلْ حُبَّكَ
اَحَبَّ اِلَىَّ مِنْ نَفْسِىْ وَاَهْلِىْ وَمِنَ الْمَاءِ الْبَارِدِ ـ

« ترمذى كتاب الدعوات »

10. Abu Darda, God be pleased with him, narrates that the Holy Prophet, peace and blessings of Allah be upon him, said that prophet David, peace be on him, used to pray in the following words:

"0 Lord, grant me Thy love and the love of those who love Thee; and the love of the deeds which will enable me to attain to Thy love. 0 my Lord, make Thy love dearer to me than my own life, my kith and kin, and even dearer than cold water (to a man dying of thirst in scorching heat)." *(Tirmidhi)*

١١ - عَنْ أَنَسٍ رضى الله عنه عَنِ النَّبِىِّ ﷺ قَالَ : ثَلَاثٌ مَنْ كُنَّ
فِيْهِ وَجَدَ بِهِنَّ حَلَاوَةَ الْاِيْمَانِ : اَنْ يَكُوْنَ اللّٰهُ وَرَسُوْلُهُ اَحَبَّ
اِلَيْهِ مِمَّا سِوَاهُمَا وَاَنْ يُحِبَّ الْمَرْءَ لَايُحِبُّهُ اِلَّا لله ، وَاَنْ يَكْرَهَ اَنْ
يَعُوْدَ فِى الْكُفْرِ بَعْدَ اَنْ اَنْقَذَهُ اللّٰهُ مِنْهُ كَمَايَكْرَهُ اَنْ يُقْذَفَ فِى
النَّارِ ـ

« بخارى كتاب الايمان باب حلاوة الايمان »

11. Anas, God be pleased with him, relates that the Holy Prophet, peace and blessings of Allah be upon him, said:

"There are three qualities which, when possessed by someone

will enable him to discover the true sweetness of faith: That Allah and His messenger are dearer to him than anything else; that he loves someone purely for the sake of Allah; that after Allah The Almighty has saved him from disbelief, he loathes returning to disbelief as much as he abhors being hurled into fire." *(Bukhari)*

١٢ ـ عَنْ أَبِيْ هُرَيْرَةَ رضى الله عنه أَنَّ رَسُوْلَ الله ﷺ قَالَ : لَوْ يَعْلَمُ الْمُؤْمِنُ مَاعِنْدَ الله مِنَ الْعُقُوْبَةِ مَاطمِحَ بِجَنَّتِهِ أَحَدٌ ، وَلَوْ يَعْلَمُ الْكَافِرُ مَا عِنْدَ الله مِنَ الرَّحْمَةِ مَا قَنَطَ مِنْ جَنَّتِهِ أَحَدٌ ـ

« مسلم كتاب التوبة باب فى سعة رحمة الله »

12. Abu Hurairah, God be pleased with him, narrates that the Holy Prophet, peace and blessings of Allah be upon him, said:

"If a believer were truly aware of the extent and intensity of God's punishment, he would lose all hope of attaining paradise. And if a disbeliever knew of the overwhelming mercy of Allah, he would never despair of paradise." *(Muslim)*

١٣ ـ عَنْ وَائِلَةَ بْنِ الاَسْقَعِ عَنِ النَّبِىِّ ﷺ قَالَ قَالَ اللَّهُ تَبَارَكَ وَ تَعَالى : اَنَا عِنْدَ ظَنِّ عَبْدِىْ بِىْ فَلْيَظُنَّ بِىْ مَاشَاءَ ـ

« بخـارى كتاب التوحيد باب يحذركم الله نفسه و مسند دارمى باب حسن الظَّنّ »

13. Waathila, God be pleased with him, narrates that the Holy Prophet, peace and blessings of Allah be upon him, said that Allah The Almighty says:

"I treat My servant in accordance with his understanding and expectations of Me. So, let him think of Me as he chooses." *(Bukhari)*

١٤ - عَنْ أَبِىْ هُرَيْرَةَ رضى الله عنه عَنْ رَسُوْلِ اللهِ ﷺ أَنَّهُ قَالَ :

قَالَ اللهُ عَزَّوَجَلَّ : اَنَا عِنْدَ ظَنِّ عَبْدِىْ بِىْ وَاَنَا مَعَهُ حَيْثُ يَذْكُرُنِى وَاللهِ اَللهُ اَفْرَحُ بِتَوْبَةِ عَبْدِهِ مِنْ اَحَدِكُمْ يَجِدُ ضَالَّتَهُ بِالْفَلَاةِ وَمَنْ تَقَرَّبَ اِلَىَّ شِبْرًا تَقَرَّبْتُ اِلَيْهِ ذِرَاعًا ، وَمَنْ تَقَرَّبَ اِلَىَّ ذِرَاعًا تَقَرَّبْتُ اِلَيْهِ بَاعًا ، وَاِذَا اَقْبَلَ اِلَىَّ يَمْشِىْ اَقْبَلْتُ اِلَيْهِ اُهَرْوِلُ ۔

« مسلم كتاب التوبة باب فى الحضّ على التوبة »

14. Abu Hurairah, God be pleased with him, narrates that the Holy Prophet, peace and blessings of Allah be upon him, conveyed that Allah The Almighty says:

'I treat My servant in accordance with his understanding of Me. I am with him whenever he remembers Me.' Allah is more pleased with the repentance of a servant of His than one of you would be if he were to lose his camel in a barren desert and then find it unexpectedly. Allah says: 'Whoever moves towards Me by the span of an open hand, 1 move towards him by half an arm's length. And whoever moves towards Me by half an arm's length, I move towards him by the length of an arm. When he comes walking towards Me, I run to meet him.' *(Muslim)*

عَنْ اَبِىْ هُرَيْرَةَ عَنْ رَسُوْلِ اللهِ ﷺ قَالَ اَسْرَفَ رَجُلٌ عَلَى - ١٥
نَفْسِهِ فَلَمَّا حَضَرَهُ الْمَوْتُ اَوْصٰى بَنِيْهِ فَقَالَ اِذَا اَنَا مَتُّ
فَاَحْرِقُوْنِىْ ثُمَّ اسْحَقُوْنِىْ ثُمَّ ذَرُوْنِىْ فِى الرِّيْحِ فِى الْبَحْرِ
فَوَاللهِ لَئِنْ قَدَرَ عَلَىَّ رَبِّىْ لَيُعَذِّبُنِىْ عَذَابًا مَّا عَذَّبَهُ اَحَدًا قَالَ
فَفَعَلُوْابِهِ ذٰلِكَ فَقَالَ لِلْاَرْضِ اَدِّىْ مَا اَخَذْتِ فَاِذَا هُوَ قَائِمٌ
فَقَالَ لَهُ : مَاحَمَلَكَ عَلٰى مَاصَنَعْتَ قَالَ : خَشْيَتُكَ اَوْ مَخَافَتُكَ
يَا رَبِّ ! فَغَفَرَلَهُ ـ

« بخارى كتاب التوحيد-ابن ماجه كتاب الزهد باب ذكر
الذنوب / مسند احمد ٢٦٩/٢ »

15. Abu Hurairah, God be pleased with him, narrates that the Holy Prophet, peace and blessings of Allah be upon him, said:

"Once there was a man who committed excesses against his ownself. When he was about to die, he told his sons, 'Burn my body when I am dead, pulverize my remains into powder, then go to the ocean and throw the ashes into the wind. I swear by Allah, I fear that if God gets hold of me, He would inflict a punishment on me which has not been inflicted upon anyone before.' Then the Holy Prophet, peace and blessings of Allah be upon him, said that the sons did as they had been told. But God ordered the earth to retrieve and return to all the particles that belonged to the man's body from wherever they had fallen. Thus the man was brought before God. Allah asked him, 'What made you do that?' He answered, 'My awe and fear of Thee forced me to do it.' So God forgave him." *(Bukhari)*

The Holy Qur'an

١٦ ـ عَنْ عُثْمَانَ بْنِ عَفَّانَ رضى الله عنه قَالَ : قَالَ رَسُوْلُ اللهِ ﷺ :
خَيْرُكُمْ مَنْ تَعَلَّمَ الْقُرْاٰنَ وَ عَلَّمَهُ ـ

« بخارى كتاب فضائل القران باب خيركم من تعلم
القران »

16. Uthman bin Affan, God be pleased with him, states that the Holy Prophet, peace and blessings of Allah be upon him, said:

"The best among you is the one who learns the Qur'an and teaches it to others." *(Bukhari)*

١٧ ـ عَن ابْنِ عَبَّاسٍ رضى الله عنها قَالَ : قَالَ رَسُوْلُ اللهِ ﷺ :
اِنَّ الَّذِىْ لَيْسَ فِىْ جَوْفِهِ شَىْءٌ مِّنَ الْقُرْاٰنِ كَالْبَيْتِ الْخَرِبِ ـ

« ترمذى فضائل القران باب من قرأ حرفا »

17. Ibn Abbas, God be pleased with him, states that the Holy Prophet, peace and blessings of Allah be upon him, said:

"The case of one who does not learn any portion of the Qur'an is like that of an abandoned house." *(Tirmidhi)*

عَنْ زَيْدِ بْنِ اَرْقَمَ قَالَ قَامَ رَسُوْلُ الله ﷺ يَوْمًا فِيْنَا خَطِيْبًا فَحَمِدَ اللهَ وَاَثْنَى عَلَيْهِ وَوَعَظَ وَ ذَكَّرَ ثُمَّ قَالَ : اَمَّا بَعْدُ اَلاَ اَيُّهَا النَّاسُ فَاِنَّمَا اَنَابَشَرٌيُوْشِكُ اَنْ يَاتِيَ رَسُوْلُ رَبِّيْ فَاُجِيْبَ وَاَنَا تَارِكٌ فِيْكُمْ ثَقَلَيْنِ اَوَّلُهُمَا كِتَابُ اللهِ فِيْهِ الْهُدَى وَالنُّوْرُ فَخُذُوْا بِكِتَابِ اللهِ وَاسْتَمْسِكُوْا بِهِ فَحَثَّ عَلَى كِتَابِ اللهِ وَ رَغَّبَ فِيْهِ ثُمَّ قَالَ : وَاَهْـلُ بَيْتِىْ ، اُذَكِّـرُكُمُ اللهَ فِىْ اَهْلِ بَيْتِىْ ، اُذَكِّرُكُمُ اللهَ فِىْ اَهْلِ بَيْتِىْ ، اُذَكِّرُكُمُ اللهَ فِىْ اَهْلِ بَيْتِىْ -

« مسلم كتاب فضائل الصحابة باب من فضائل على »

18. Zaid bin Arqam, God be pleased with him, narrates:

"One day, the Holy Prophet, peace and blessings of Allah be upon him, stood to address us: he praised Allah, glorified Him, and then exhorted and admonished us, saying:

'0 people! I am a human being. It is likely that one day a messenger from my Lord will come to me, and then I will depart from this world. I am leaving two important things among you: the Book of Allah, containing guidance and light. So, hold fast to the Book of Allah and abide by it.'

Thus he aroused our interest and made us excited about the Book of Allah. Then he said: 'I am also leaving behind the members of my household.'

He then said three times, 'I caution you to be mindful of Allah as to how you treat my family members.' *(Muslim)*

The Excellent Conduct of the Messenger of Allah

١٩ - عَنْ عَبْدِاللهِ بْنِ اَبِىْ اَوْفٰى قَالَ: كَانَ النَّبِىُّ ﷺ لَايَأْنَفُ وَلَا يَسْتَنْكِفُ اَنْ يَّمْشِىَ مَعَ الْاَرْمَلَةِ وَالْمِسْكِيْنِ فَيَقْضِىْ لَهُمَا حَاجَتَهُمَا ـ

« مسند دارمى باب فى تواضع رسول الله صلى الله عليه وسلم »

19. Abdullah bin Abi Aufa, God be pleased with him, said:

"The Holy Prophet, peace and blessings of Allah be upon him, neither scorned nor shunned the company of widows and the needy; on the contrary, he always sought opportunities to help them." *(Musnad Darmi)*

٢٠ - عَنْ عَائِشَةَ رضى الله عنها قَالَتْ مَاضَرَبَ رَسُوْلُ اللهِ ﷺ شَيْئًاقَطُّ بِيَدِهِ وَلَا امْرَأَةً وَلَا خَادِمًا اِلَّا اَنْ يُّجَاهِدَ فِىْ سَبِيْلِ اللهِ وَمَانِيْلَ مِنْهُ شَيْئٌ قَطُّ فَيَنْتَقِمَ مِنْ صَاحِبِهِ اِلَّا اَنْ يُّنْتَهَكَ شَىْءٌ مِنْ مَحَارِمِ اللهِ فَيَنْتَقِمَ لِلّٰهِ عَزَّوَجَلَّ ـ

« مسلم كتاب الفضائل باب مباعدته الآثام واختياره من المباح »

20. Ayesha, God be pleased with her, states:

"The Holy Prophet, peace and blessings of Allah be upon him, never beat anyone, neither a woman nor a servant, although he fought in the cause of Allah. If he was ever harmed by anyone, he would not avenge himself. But whenever a sacred place of Allah was desecrated, he would take revenge for the sake of Allah."

(Muslim)

عَنْ أَبِى سَعِيْدٍ الْخُدْرِىِّ رضى الله عنه أَنَّ رَسُوْلَ اللهِ ﷺ كَانَ يَعْلِفُ الْبَعِيْرَ وَيُقِيْمُ الْبَيْتَ وَيَخْصِفُ النَّعْلَ وَيَرْفَعُ الثَّوْبَ وَيَحْلُبُ الشَّاةَ وَيَاكُلُ مَعَ الْخَادِمِ وَيَطْحَنُ مَعَهُ اِذَا أَعْيَا وَكَانَ لَايَمْنَعُهُ الْحَيَاءُ اَنْ يَحْمِلَ بِضَاعَتَهُ مِنَ السُّوْقِ اِلَى اَهْلِهِ وَكَانَ يُصَافِحُ الْغَنِىَّ وَالْفَقِيْرَ وَيُسَلِّمُ مُبْتَدِيًا وَلَايَحْتَقِرُ مَا دُعِىَ اِلَيْهِ وَلَوْ اِلَى حَشْفِ التَّمْرِ وَكَانَ هَيِّنَ الْمُؤْنَةِ ، لَيِّنَ الْخُلُقِ ، كَرِيْمَ الطَّبِيْعَةِ ، جَمِيْلَ الْمُعَاشَرَةِ ، طَلِقَ الْوَجْهِ ، بَسَّامًا مِنْ غَيْرِ ضِحْكٍ ، مَحْزُوْنًا مِنْ غَيْرِ عُبُوْسَةٍ ، مُتَوَاضِعًا مِنْ غَيْرِ مَذلَّةٍ ، جَوَادًا مِنْ غَيْرِ سَرَفٍ رَقِيْقَ الْقَلْبِ رَحِيْمًا بِكُلِّ مُسْلِمٍ لَمْ يَتَجَشَّأْقَطُ مِنْ شَبَعٍ وَلَمْ يَمُدَّ يَدَهُ اِلَى طَمَعٍ ـ

« مشكوة كتاب الفتن باب فى اخلاقه ـ قشيريه ص ٧٥
اسدالغابة جلد اول ص « ٢٩ »

21. Abu Saeed Khudri, God be pleased with him, narrates:

"The Holy Prophet, peace and blessings of Allah be upon him, used to feed the camels himself: He would perform household chores: mend shoes, darn clothes, milk goats, and eat in the company of servants. If a servant became tired while grinding flour, he would help him at this. He would not feel belittled carrying household goods from the market to the house. He would shake hands with the rich and the poor alike. He would always be the first to extend greetings. He would not disdain accepting an invitation not even so small an invitation as to join in eating dates. He would relieve those who toiled. He was mild tempered and kind hearted. His conduct was excellent and he was always cheerful. He would smile but would not laugh loudly; he would not frown even when vexed. He was humble, but not lowly; generous, but not extravagant. He was tender hearted and merciful to all Muslims alike. He would never eat his fill to the point where one is likely to start yawning. He would never extend his hand motivated by greed." *(Mishkaat)*

٢٢ - عَنْ اَبِیْ مُوْسَی الْاَشْعَرِیَّ رضی الله عنه قَالَ : اَخْرَجَتْ لَنَا عَائِشَةُ رضی الله عنها كِسَاءً وَاِزَارًا غَلِیْظًا قَالَتْ : قُبِضَ رَسُوْلُ الله ﷺ فِیْ هٰذَیْنِ ۔

« بخاری کتاب اللباس باب الاکسیۃ »

22. Abu Musa Ashari, God be pleased with him, narrates that once Ayesha, God be pleased with her, showed them a sheet and a loin, cloth made of thick rough fabric. She said that the Holy Prophet, peace and blessings of Allah be upon him, was wearing these clothes at the time of his demise.   *(Bukhari)*

The Foundations of Islam

٢٣ ـ عَنْ ابْنِ عُمَرَ رضى الله عنهما قَالَ : قَالَ رَسُوْلُ الله ﷺ : بُنِيَ الْإِسْلَامُ عَلَى خَمْسٍ : شَهَادَةِ اَنْ لَّا اِلٰهَ اِلَّا اللهُ وَاَنَّ مُحَمَّدًا رَسُوْلُ الله وَاِقَامِ الصَّلٰوةِ ، وَاِيْتَاءِ الـزَّكٰوةِ ، وَحَجِّ الْبَيْتِ ، وَصَوْمِ رَمَضَانَ ـ

« بخارى كتاب الايمان باب قول النبى صلى الله عليه وسلم بنى الاسلام »

23. Ibn Umar, God be pleased with him, relates that the Holy Prophet, peace and blessings of Allah be upon him, said:

"Islam is based on five pillars:

1. To bear witness that none is worthy of worship except Allah and that Muhammad is the Messenger of Allah.
2. To offer the Salat (The formal way of worshipping God).
3. To pay the Zakat (The obligatory, minimum requirements of financial contribution in the cause of Allah).
4. To perform the pilgrimage to the House of Allah.
5. To keep the fast in the month of Ramadhan." *(Bukhari)*

٢٤ ـ عَنْ عُمَرَبْنِ الْخَطَّابِ رضى الله عنه قَالَ كُنَّاعِنْدَ رَسُوْلِ الله ﷺ فَجَاءَ رَجُلٌ شَدِيْدُ بَيَاضِ الثِّيَابِ شَدِيْدُ سَوَادِ الشَّعْرِ لَايُرٰى عَلَيْهِ اَثَرُالسَّفَرِ وَلَا يَعْرِفُهُ مِنَّا اَحَدٌ حَتّٰى اَتَى النَّبِيَّ ﷺ فَاَلْزَقَ رُكْبَتَهُ بِرُكْبَتِهِ ثُمَّ قَالَ يَا مُحَمَّدُ مَا الْاِيْمَانُ قَالَ اَنْ تُؤْمِنَ بِالله وَمَلَائِكَتِهِ وَكُتُبِهِ وَرُسُلِهِ وَالْيَوْمِ الْاخِرِ وَالْقَدْرِ خَيْرِهِ وَشَرِّهِ ـ

« ترمذى كتاب الايمان باب فى وصف جبريل النبى صلى الله عليه وسلم الايمان والاسلام »

24. Omar bin Khattab, God be pleased with him, says:

"We were sitting in the company of the Holy Prophet, peace and blessings of Allah be upon him, when suddenly a man arrived. He was wearing clean, white clothes and his hair was jet black. He did not look as though he were a traveller and he was not known to any of us. He sat down close to the Holy Prophet, peace and blessings of Allah be upon him, his knees touching the latter's. He said, 'Tell me something about faith.' The Holy Prophet, peace and blessings of Allah be upon him, replied: 'Faith is that you should believe in Allah, His angels, His Books and His prophets; that you should believe in the Day of judgment and that you should believe in the Divine laws relating to good and evil.'

(Tirmidhi)

٢٥ ـ عَنْ عُثْمَانَ بْنِ عَفَّانَ رضى الله عنه اَنَّهُ دَعَا بِاِنَاءٍ فَاَفْرَغَ عَلَى كَفَّيْهِ ثَلثَ مِرَارٍ فَغَسَلَهُمَا ثُمَّ اَدْخَلَ يَمِيْنَهُ فِى الاِنَآءِ فَمَضْمَضَ وَاسْتَنْثَرَ ثُمَّ غَسَلَ وَجْهَهُ ثَلثًا وَيَدَيْهِ اِلَى الْمِرْفَقَيْنِ ثَلثَ مِرَارٍ ثُمَّ مَسَحَ بِرَأْسِهِ ثُمَّ غَسَلَ رِجْلَيْهِ ثَلثَ مِرَارٍ اِلَى الْكَعْبَيْنِ ثُمَّ قَالَ قَالَ رَسُوْلُ الله ﷺ : مَنْ تَوَضَّأَ نَحْوَ وُضُوْئِىْ هٰذَا ثُمَّ صَلَّى رَكْعَتَيْنِ لَايُحْدِثُ فِيْهِمَا غُفِرَلَهُ مَاتَقَدَّمَ مِنْ ذَنْبِهِ ـ

« بخارى كتاب الوضوء باب الوضوء ثلثًاثلثًا »

25. It is reported that once Uthman bin Affan, God be pleased with him, asked for water (so that he could perform ablution, which is a precondition for performing salat). He began by washing his hands three times; then, taking some water in his right hand, he rinsed his mouth and spat it out; then he cleansed his nose; then he washed his face three times; he then washed his hands and forearms up to his elbows three times; after this he passed his wet hands over his head; then he washed his feet up to his ankles three times. After completing his ablution in this manner, he said:

"The Holy Prophet, peace and blessings of Allah be upon him, said that the one who performs the ablution in the manner that I did and then offers two rakats of prayer exactly as I do without making innovations, will have his past sins forgiven." *(Bukhari)*

٢٦ ـ عَنْ أَبِي هُرَيْرَةَ رضى الله عنه أَنَّ رَسُوْلَ الله ﷺ قَالَ: اَلَا
أَدُلُّكُمْ عَلى مَايَمْحُو اللهُ بِهِ الْخَطَايَا، وَيَرْفَعُ بِهِ الدَّرَجَاتِ؟
قَالُـوْا: بَلى يَارَسُوْلَ الله، قَالَ: اِسْبَـاغُ الْـوُضُـوْءِ عَلَى
الْمَكَارِهِ، وَكَثْرَةُ الْخُطَا اِلَى الْمَسَاجِدِ، وَانْتِظَارُ الصَّلوةِ بَعْدَ
الصَّلوةِ، فَذلِكُمُ الرِّبَاطُ، فَذلِكُمُ الرِّبَاطُ ـ

« مسلم كتاب الطهارات باب فضل اسباغ الوضوء على
المكاره »

26. Abu Hurairah, God be pleased with him, narrates that the Holy Prophet, peace and blessings of Allah be upon him, said:

"Should I not tell you of something which if you practice it will earn you Allah's favour and by means of which Allah will expunge your faults and elevate your rank?

They said: "0 Prophet of Allah, please do tell us." The Holy Prophet, peace and blessings of Allah be upon him, said,' 'To perform the ablution thoroughly even though one may not feel like it; to walk to the mosque from a distant place; and, having offered one's prayers, to await the next prayer eagerly. These are the means of being in a state of readiness to guard the frontiers."

(Muslim)

[Note: The word *'ribaat'* covers a wide range of meaning: it literally means geographical frontiers and metaphorically applies to any spiritual value. In this case it applies to the institution of worship in Islam.]

عَنْ عَائِشَةَ رضى الله عنها قَالَتْ : كَانَ رَسُولُ اللهِ ﷺ يَفْتَتِحُ
الصَّلَاةَ بِالتَّكْبِيرِ وَالْقِرَأَةِ بِالْحَمْدِ للهِ رَبِّ الْعَالَمِيْنَ ـ وَكَانَ اِذَا
رَكَعَ لَمْ يَرْفَعْ رَأْسَهُ وَلَمْ يُصَوِّبْهُ وَلَكِنْ بَيْنَ ذٰلِكَ وَكَانَ اِذَا
رَفَعَ رَأْسَهُ مِنَ الرُّكُوْعِ لَمْ يَسْجُدْ حَتّى يَسْتَوِىَ قَائِمًا ـ
وَاِذَا رَفَعَ رَأْسَهُ مِنَ السُّجُوْدِ لَمْ يَسْجُدْ حَتّى يَسْتَوِىَ جَالِسًا ـ
وَكَانَ يَقُوْلُ فِىْ كُلِّ رَكْعَتَيْنِ التَّحِيَّةَ وَكَانَ يَفْرِشُ رِجْلَهُ
الْيُسْرَى وَيَنْصُبُ رِجْلَهُ الْيُمْنَى وَكَانَ يَنْهى عَنْ عَقِبِ
الشَّيْطَانِ وَكَانَ يَنْهى أَنْ يَفْتَرِشَ الرَّجُلُ ذِرَاعَيْهِ افْتِرَاشَ
الْكَلْبِ وَكَانَ يَخْتِمُ الصَّلٰوةَ بِالتَّسْلِيْمِ ـ

« مسند احمد ٦/٣١ »

27. Ayesha, God be pleased with her, narrates:

"The Holy Prophet, peace and blessings of Allah be upon him, would say the takbeer (the words: *Allaho Akbar*) at the beginning of the prayer. After this, he would recite the *Fatiha* (the first chapter of the Holy Quran). When he bowed down, he would not keep his head high nor would he let it droop. Rather he would keep it in a straight line with his back which stayed horizontal during this posture. When he rose from the bowing position, he would stand upright and then move into the prostrate position. When he raised his head from the prostrate position, he would assume a sitting position and pause a while before going into the second prostration. After every two Rakats he would sit down to recite the *Attahiyat* (a prescribed recitation). In this posture his right foot was placed vertically and his left foot rested horizontally on the ground. He instructed, 'Do not rest your elbows on the ground during prostration in the manner of a dog.' And he forbade stretching the legs in a devilish posture. He would end the prayer saying, 'Peace and mercy of Allah be upon you.' (*Musnad Ahmad*)

عَنْ عَبْدِاللهِ بْنِ مَسْعُودٍ رضى الله عنه قَالَ : سَأَلْتُ النَّبِيَّ ﷺ
اَىُّ الْعَمَلِ اَحَبُّ اِلَى اللهِ تَعَالَى ؟ قَالَ : اَلصَّلوةُ عَلَى وَقْتِهَا ،
قُلْتُ : ثُمَّ اَىُّ ؟ قَالَ : بِرُّالْوَالِدَيْنِ ، قُلْتُ : ثُمَّ اَىُّ ؟ قَالَ :
اَلْجِهَادُ فِىْ سَبِيْلِ اللهِ ۔

« بخارى كتاب الجهاد باب فضل الجهاد والسير »

28. Abdullah bin Masud, God be pleased with him, states that he
asked the Holy Prophet, peace and blessings of Allah be upon him,
which deed was most pleasing to Allah The Exalted. The Holy
Prophet replied:

"'Offering the prayers at the appointed time.' I enquired, 'And
after this?' He replied, 'Being kind to parents.' I asked, 'Which
deed after this?' He answered, 'Striving in the path of Allah.'
(Bukhari)

عَنْ عَمْرِوبْنِ شُعَيْبٍ عَنْ اَبِيهِ عَنْ جَدِّهِ رضى الله عنهم
قَالَ : قَالَ رَسُوْلُ اللهِ ﷺ مُرُوْا اَوْلَادَكُمْ بِالصَّلوةِ وَهُمْ اَبْنَاءُ
سَبْعِ سِنِيْنَ وَاضْرِبُوْهُمْ عَلَيْهَا وَهُمْ اَبْنَاءُ عَشْرٍ وَفَرِّقُوْا
بَيْنَهُمْ فِى الْمَضَاجِعِ ۔

« ابوداؤد باب متى يؤمر الغلام بالصلوة ۔ مسند احمد
٢ / ١٨٠ »

29. Amar bin Shuaib, God be pleased with him, heard from his
father on the authority of his grandfather that the Holy Prophet,
peace and blessings of Allah be upon him, said:

"Advise your children to perform the prayers when they reach
the age of seven. When they reach the age of ten, you should be
strict with them in this matter, and you should also make them
sleep in separate beds." (Abu Dawood)

عَنْ فَاطِمَةَ الزَّهْرَاءِ رضى الله عنها قَالَتْ : كَانَ رَسُوْلُ اللهِ ﷺ اذَا دَخَلَ الْمَسْجِدَ قَالَ : بِسْمِ اللهِ وَالسَّلَامُ عَلَى رَسُوْلِ اللهِ ، اَللّٰهُمَّ اغْفِرْلِيْ ذُنُوْبِيْ وَافْتَحْ لِيْ اَبْوَابَ رَحْمَتِكَ وَاِذَا خَرَجَ قَالَ : بِسْمِ اللهِ وَالسَّلَامُ عَلَى رَسُوْلِ اللهِ ، اَللّٰهُمَّ اغْفِرْلِيْ ذُنُوْبِيْ وَافْتَحْ لِيْ اَبْوَابَ فَضْلِكَ ـ

« مسند احمد حديث فاطمه بنت رسول الله صلى الله عليه وسلم ص ٢٨٣ / ٦ »

30. Fatimah az Zahra, God be pleased with her, narrates that when the Holy Prophet, peace and blessings of Allah be upon him, entered the mosque, he would recite the following prayer:

"In the name of Allah; peace be on the Messenger of Allah. O, my Lord forgive me my sins, and open the gates of Thy mercy to me."

And when he departed from the mosque, he would offer the following prayer:

"In the name of Allah; peace be upon the Messenger of Allah. Forgive me my sins, my Lord and open the gates of Thy grace to me."   *(Musnad Ahmad)*

Fasting

٣١ - عَنْ أَبِىْ هُرَيْرَةَ رضى الله عنه قَالَ : قَالَ رَسُوْلُ الله ﷺ :
قَالَ اللَّهُ عَزَّوَجَلَّ : كُلُّ عَمَلِ ابْنِ اٰدَمَ لَهُ اِلَّا الصِّيَامَ فَاِنَّهُ لِىْ
وَاَنَا اَجْزِىْ بِهِ وَالصِّيَامُ جُنَّةٌ فَاِذَا كَانَ يَوْمُ صَوْمِ اَحَدِكُمْ فَلَا
يَرْفُثْ وَلَا يَصْخَبْ فَاِنْ سَابَّهُ اَحَدٌ اَوْ قَاتَلَهُ فَلْيَقُلْ : اِنِّىْ
صَائِمٌ ، وَالَّذِىْ نَفْسُ مُحَمَّدٍ بِيَدِهِ لَخُلُوْفُ فَمِ الصَّائِمِ
اَطْيَبُ عِنْدَ الله مِنْ رِيْحِ الْمِسْكِ ـ لِلصَّائِمِ فَرْحَتَانِ
يَفْرَحُهُمَا : اِذَا اَفْطَرَ فَرِحَ وَاِذَا لَقِىَ رَبَّهُ فَرِحَ بِصَوْمِهٖ ـ

« بخارى كتاب الصوم باب هل يقول انى صائم اذا شتم »

31. Abu Hurairah, God be pleased with him, narrates that the Holy Prophet, peace and blessings of Allah be upon him, said:

"Allah The Almighty says that all the deeds of a man are for his own sake except the fast. 'The fast is kept for My sake alone, and I am the reward for it.' The fast is a shield against evil. Thus, when anyone of you is fasting, he should neither indulge in idle talk nor raise his voice. If anyone abuses him or starts quarreling with him, he should just say, 'I am fasting.' Let Allah the Possessor of Muhammad and his life bear me out: the breath of one who is fasting is purer in the sight of Allah than the fragrance of musk. One who fasts experiences two joys: he is joyful when he breaks the fast, and he is joyful by virtue of the fast when he meets his Lord." *(Bukhari)*

٣٢ـ عَنْ اَبِىْ هُرَيْرَةَ رضى الله عنه قَالَ : قَالَ النَّبِىُّ ﷺ : مَنْ لَمْ
يَدَعْ قَوْلَ الـزُّوْرِ وَالْعَمَلَ بِهِ فَلَيْسَ لله حَاجَةٌ فِىْ اَنْ يَدَعَ
طَعَامَهُ وَشَرَابَهُ ـ

« بخـارى كتـاب الصـوم بـاب من لم يدع قول الزور و
العمل به »

32. Abu Hurairah, God be pleased with him, narrates, that the
Holy Prophet, peace and blessings of Allah be upon him, said:

"Of what use to Allah is the fast of one who does not abstain
from lying and from deceit."   *(Bukhari)*

٣٣ـ عَنْ عَآئِشَةَ رضى الله عنها اَنَّ النَّبِىَّ ﷺ كَانَ يَعْتَكِفُ
الْعَشْرَ الْاَوَاخِـرَ مِنْ رَمَضَـانَ حَتَّى تَوَفَّـاهُ اللَّهُ تَعَـالىٰ ثُمَّ
اعْتَكَفَ اَزْوَاجُهُ مِنْ بَعْدِه

« بخارى كتاب الاعتكاف باب الاعتكاف فى العشر
الاواخر »

33. Ayesha, God be pleased with her, narrates that the Holy
Prophet, peace and blessings of Allah be upon him, would remain
confined to the mosque *(Etikaf)* for the last ten days of the month
of Ramadhan. After his demise, his wives continued to observe the
(Etikaf) in the same manner.   *(Bukhari)*

The Hajj

٣٤ ـ عَنْ اَبِىْ هُرَيْرَةَ رضى الله عنه قَالَ خَطَبَنَا رَسُوْلُ اللهِ ﷺ
فَقَالَ : يَاَيُّهَا النَّاسُ اِنَّ اللهَ قَدْ فَرَضَ عَلَيْكُمُ الْحَجَّ فَحُجُّوْا
فَقَالَ رَجُلٌ : اَكُلَّ عَامٍ يَارَسُوْلَ اللهِ ؟ فَسَكَتَ حَتَّى قَالَهَا
ثَلاَثًا ـ فَقَالَ رَسُوْلُ اللهِ ﷺ لَوْ قُلْتُ نَعَمْ لَوَجَبَتْ
وَلَمَااسْتَطَعْتُمْ ثُمَّ قَالَ : ذَرُوْنِىْ مَاتَرَكْتُكُمْ فَاِنَّمَا هَلَكَ مَنْ كَانَ
قَبْلَكُمْ بِكَثْرَةِ سُؤَالِهِمْ ، وَاخْتِلاَفِهِمْ عَلَى اَنْبِيَائِهِمْ ، فَاِذَا
اَمَرْتُكُمْ بِشَىءٍ فَأْتُوْامِنْهُ مَااسْتَطَعْتُمْ وَاِذَا نَهَيْتُكُمْ عَنْ شَىءٍ
فَدَعُوْهُ ـ

« مسلم كتاب الحج باب فرض الحج مرة فى العمر »

34. Abu Hurairah, God be pleased with him, narrates that the Holy Prophet, peace and blessings of Allah be upon him, while delivering a sermon, stated:

"0 people! Allah has made the pilgrimage obligatory upon you. So you should perform it."

Hearing this a man asked, 'Is it to be performed every year, 0 Prophet of Allah?' The Holy Prophet, peace and blessings of Allah be upon him, kept silent. The man put his question three times. The Holy Prophet, peace and blessings of Allah be upon him, then replied: "If I say 'yes', it would become obligatory, and you would not have the strength for that."

He continued, "Do not inquire about something so long as I do not tell you about it. Those before you were destroyed because they asked too many questions but disobeyed the prophets. When I command you to do something, you should perform it to the best of your ability. And if I forbid you to do something, you should abstain from it." *(Muslim)*

٣٥ ـ عَنْ أَبِى هُرَيْرَةَ قَالَ قَالَ رَسُولُ اللهِ صَلَّى اللهُ عَلَيْهِ وَسَلَّمَ مَنْ حَجَّ لِلّهِ فَلَمْ يَرْفُثْ وَلَمْ يَفْسُقْ رَجَعَ كَيَوْمٍ وَلَدَتْهُ أُمُّهُ ـ

« مِشْكوٰةِ كِتَابُ الْمَنَاسِك »

35. Abu Hurairah, God be pleased with him, narrates that the Holy Prophet, peace and blessings of Allah be upon him, said:

"When someone performs the pilgrimage for the sake of Allah, and does not indulge in foul talk or commit any transgression, he becomes as pure and innocent as the day his mother gave birth to him." *(Mishkat)*

The Zakaat

(Spending in the Way of Allah)

٣٦ ـ عَنْ مُعَاذٍ رضى الله عنه قَالَ بَعَثَنِىْ رَسُوْلُ اللهِ ﷺ فَقَالَ :
اِنَّكَ تَأْتِىْ قَوْمًا مِّنْ اَهْلِ الْكِتَابِ فَادْعُهُمْ اِلىٰ شَهَادَةِ اَنْ لَّا
اِلـٰهَ اِلَّا اللّٰهُ وَ اَنِّىْ رَسُـوْلُ اللهِ ، فَاِنْ هُمْ اَطَاعُوْا لِذٰلِكَ
فَاَعْلِمْهُمْ اَنَّ اللهَ قَدِ افْتَرَضَ عَلَيْهِمْ خَمْسَ صَلَوَاتٍ فْىْ كُلِّ
يَوْمٍ وَّلَيْلَةٍ ، فَاِنْ هُمْ اَطَاعُوْا لِذٰلِكَ فَاَعْلِمْهُمْ اَنَّ اللهَ قَدِ
افْــتَرَضَ عَلَيْهِمْ صَدَقَةً تُوْخَـذُ مِنْ اَغْنِيَـآئِهِمْ فَتُرَدُّ عَلىٰ
فُقَرَائِهِمْ فَاِنْ هُمْ اَطَـاعُوْا لِذٰلِكَ فَاِيَّاكَ وَكَرَائِمَ اَمْوَالِهِمْ ـ
وَاتَّقِ دَعْوَةَ الْمَظْلُومِ فَاِنَّهُ لَيْسَ بَيْنَهَا وَ بَيْنَ اللهِ حِجَابٌ ـ
« بخارى كتاب الزكوة باب لاتؤخذ كرائم اموال الناس فى
الصدقة »

36. Muaz, God be pleased with him, narrates:

"Having appointed me governor (of a region), the Holy
Prophet, peace and blessings of Allah be upon him, sent for me
and told me: 'You will meet some People of the Book. You
should invite them to bear witness that there is none worthy of
worship except Allah and that I am His Messenger. If they accept
this, you should let them know that Allah has made it obligatory to
offer the five daily prayers. If they accept this, you should tell
them that Allah has made it obligatory to give alms. These alms
are taken from the rich and returned to the poor among them. If
they agree to this, do not require the best of what they possess.
And be mindful of the plea of the oppressed because nothing
stands between this plea and Allah."   *(Bukhari)*

٣٧ - عَنْ خُرَيْمِ بْنِ فَاتِكٍ رضى الله عنه قَالَ: قَالَ رَسُوْلُ الله
ﷺ: مَنْ اَنْفَقَ نَفَقَةً فِىْ سَبِيْلِ الله كُتِبَ لَهُ سَبْعُمِأَةِ ضِعْفٍ۔

« ترمذى باب فضل النفقة فى سبيل الله »

37. Khuraim bin Fatik, God be pleased with him, narrates that the Holy Prophet, peace and blessings of Allah be upon him, said:

"Whoever spends something in the cause of Allah is rewarded seven hundred times over." *(Tirmidhi)*

٣٨ - عَنْ اَنَسٍ رضى الله عنه قَالَ: كَانَ اَبُوْطَلْحَةَ رضى الله عنه
اَكْثَرَ الْاَنْصَارِ بِالْمَدِيْنَةِ مَالًا مِنْ نَخْلٍ وَكَانَ اَحَبُّ اَمْوَالِهِ اِلَيْهِ
بَيْرُحَآءَ وَ كَانَتْ مُسْتَقْبِلَةَ الْمَسْجِدِ وَكَانَ رَسُوْلُ الله ﷺ
يَدْخُلُهَا وَ يَشْرَبُ مِنْ مَّآءٍ فِيْهَا طَيِّبٍ قَالَ اَنَسٌ فَلَمَّا نَزَلَتْ
هٰذِهِ الْآيَةُ:
لَنْ تَنَالُوا الْبِرَّ حَتّٰى تُنْفِقُوْا مِمَّا تُحِبُّوْنَ ، جَآءَ اَبُوْطَلْحَةَ اِلٰى
رَسُوْلِ الله ﷺ فَقَالَ: يَارَسُوْلَ الله اِنَّ الله تَعَالٰى اَنْزَلَ
عَلَيْكَ لَنْ تَنَالُوا الْبِرَّ حَتّٰى تُنْفِقُوْا مِمَّا تُحِبُّوْنَ ٥ وَاِنَّ اَحَبَّ مَالِىْ
اِلَىَّ بَيْرُحَآءَ وَاِنَّهَا صَدَقَةٌ لله تَعَالٰى اَرْجُوْ بِرَّهَا وَذُخْرَهَا عِنْدَ
الله تَعَالٰى فَضَعْهَا يَارَسُوْلَ الله حَيْثُ اَرَاكَ اللهُ، فَقَالَ رَسُوْلُ
الله ﷺ بَخْ! ذٰلِكَ مَالٌ رَابِحٌ، ذٰلِكَ مَالٌ رَابِحٌ وَقَدْ
سَمِعْتُ مَاقُلْتَ وَ اِنِّىْ اَرٰى اَنْ تَجْعَلَهَا فِى الْاَقْرَبِيْنَ فَقَالَ
اَبُوْطَلْحَةَ: اَفْعَلُ يَارَسُوْلَ الله، فَقَسَمَهَا اَبُوْطَلْحَةَ فِىْ
اَقَارِبِهِ وَبَنِىْ عَمِّهِ۔

« بخارى كتاب التفسير باب لن تنالوا البر حتى تنفقوا مما
تحبون »

29

38. Anas, God be pleased with him, narrates that Abu Talha Ansari was the wealthiest of the Ansar, (the people of Medina who accepted Islam before the migration of the Holy Prophet, peace and blessings of Allah be upon him, to that town). The source of his income was from date-palm gardens, and the garden most dear to him was *Bayruha*. It was situated opposite the Prophet's mosque. The Holy Prophet, peace and blessings of Allah be upon him, used to enter it and drink its pure and fresh water. Anas, God be pleased with him, says, 'When the verse: *You cannot attain to righteousness unless you spend out of that which you love'* was revealed, Abu Talha, God be pleased with him, went to the Holy Prophet, peace and blessings of Allah be upon him, and said, '0 Messenger of Allah, Allah has revealed to you: *You cannot attain to righteousness unless you spend out of that which you love',* and the dearest of my possessions is the *Bayruha* garden. I give this as charity in the cause of Allah, and hope that Allah will accept this good deed and preserve it for the Hereafter. Use it, O Messenger of Allah, as Allah directs you.' The Holy Prophet, peace and blessings of Allah be upon him, said: 'Excellent! it is a profitable asset. It is a profitable asset. 1 have heard what you propose, but I think you should give it to your relatives.' Abu Talha, God be pleased with him, said, 'I will do as you have told me, 0 Messenger of Allah.' Abu Talha, God be pleased with him, accordingly divided it between his near relatives and the children of his uncle.' *(Bukhari)*

عَنْ عَدِيِّ بْنِ حَاتِمٍ رضى الله عنه اَنَّ رَسُوْلَ اللهِ ﷺ قَالَ : ۳۹-

اتَّقُوا النَّارَ وَلَوْ بِشِقِّ تَمْرَةٍ -

« بخارى كتاب الزكوٰة باب اتقوا النار ولو بشق تمرة »

39. Adiyi bin Hatim, God be pleased with him, narrates that the Holy Prophet, peace and blessings of Allah be upon him, said.

"Give charity to save yourself from the fire even if it be by giving a portion of a date." *(Bukhari)*

٤٠ - عَنْ عَائِشَةَ رضى الله عنها قَالَتْ: قَالَ رَسُوْلُ اللهِ ﷺ:
اَلسَّخِىُّ قَرِيْبٌ مِنَ اللهِ تَعَالَى قَرِيْبٌ مِنَ النَّاسِ قَرِيْبٌ مِنَ
الْجَنَّةِ بَعِيْدٌ مِنَ النَّارِ وَالْبَخِيْلُ بَعِيْدٌ مِنَ اللهِ تَعَالَى بَعِيْدٌ مِنَ
النَّاسِ بَعِيْدٌ مِنَ الْجَنَّةِ قَرِيْبٌ مِنَ النَّارِ وَالْجَاهِلُ السَّخِىُّ
أَحَبُّ إِلَى اللهِ تَعَالَى مِنَ الْعَابِدِ الْبَخِيْلِ ـ

« قشيريه ـ الجود والسخاء »

40. Ayesha, God be pleased with her, narrates that the Holy
Prophet, peace and blessings of Allah be upon him, said:

"A generous person is close to Allah, close to the people and
close to Paradise but far away from Hell. As opposed to this, a
miser is far away from Allah, from the people and from Paradise,
but close to Hell. An ignorant person who is generous is dearer to
Allah than a worshipping miser." *(Qushariyyah)*

٤١ - عَنْ أَبِى هُرَيْرَةَ قَالَ قَالَ رَجُلٌ: يَارَسُوْلَ اللهِ! أَىُّ الصَّدَقَةِ
أَعْظَمُ أَجْرًا قَالَ: أَنْ تَصَدَّقَ وَأَنْتَ صَحِيْحٌ تَخْشَى الْفَقْرَ وَ
تَأَمَّلَ الْغِنَى وَلاَ تُمْهِلْ حَتَّى إِذَا بَلَغَتِ الْحُلْقُوْمَ قُلْتَ لِفُلَانٍ
كَذَا وَكَذَا وَقَدْ كَانَ لِفُلَانٍ ـ

« مشكوة كتاب الانفاق »

41. Abu Hurairah, God be pleased with him, narrates that a
person inquired of the Holy Prophet, peace and blessings of Allah
be upon him,

"0 Messenger of Allah, which act of charity has the greatest
reward?" The Messenger of Allah answered, 'That you give
charity when you are in good health, when you yourself stand in
need, and when you are afraid of poverty and desire to become
wealthy-if, even then, you are not neglectful. Not that you tarry
until your life is ebbing out, and then you say this much for him
and that much for him." *(Mishkat)*

Enjoining Good and Forbidding Evil

عَنْ حُذَيْفَةَ اَنَّ النَّبِيَّ ﷺ قَالَ : وَالَّذِيْ نَفْسِيْ بِيَدِهِ لَتَأْمُرُوْنَ بِالْمَعْرُوْفِ وَلَتَنْهَوْنَ عَنِ الْمُنْكَرِ اَوْلَيُوْشِكَنَّ اللهُ اَنْ يَبْعَثَ عَلَيْكُمْ عَذَابًا مِنْ عِنْدِهِ ثُمَّ لَتَدْعُنَّهُ وَلاَ يُسْتَجَابَ لَكُمْ ـ ٤٢ -

« ترمذى ابواب الفتن باب الامر بالمعروف والنهى عن المنكر »

42. Huzaifa, God be pleased with him, relates that the Holy Prophet, peace and blessings of Allah be upon him, said:

"I swear by Him who holds my life in His hands, that you must enjoin on people to do good and forbid them from doing wrong; otherwise, it is quite likely that some punishment from Allah may be inflicted upon you. Then, too late, you will offer supplications but they will not be accepted." *(Tirmidhi)*

عَنْ نُعْمَانَ بْنِ بَشِيرٍ رضى الله عنهما عَنِ النَّبِيِّ ﷺ قَالَ : مَثَلُ الْقَائِمِ عَلَى حُدُوْدِ اللهِ وَالْوَاقِعِ فِيْهَا كَمَثَلِ قَوْمٍ اسْتَهَمُوْا عَلَى سَفِيْنَةٍ فَأَصَابَ بَعْضُهُمْ اَعْلاَهَا وَبَعْضُهُمْ اَسْفَلَهَا فَكَانَ الَّذِيْنَ فِى اَسْفَلِهَا إِذَا اسْتَقَوْا مِنَ الْمَاءِ مَرُّوْا عَلَى مَنْ فَوْقَهُمْ ـ فَقَالُوْا لَوْ اَنَّا خَرَقْنَا فِىْ نَصِيْبِنَا خَرْقًا وَلَمْ نُؤْذِ مَنْ فَوْقَنَا فَاِنْ يَتْرُكُوْهُمْ وَمَا اَرَادُوْا هَلَكُوْا جَمِيْعًا وَاِنْ اَخَذُوْا عَلَى اَيْدِيْهِمْ نَجَوْا وَ نَجَوْا جَمِيْعًا ـ ٤٣ -

« بخـارى كتـاب الشـركـة بـاب هل يقـرع فى القسمة والاستهام فيه »

43. No'maan bin Basheer, God be pleased with him, related that

the Holy Prophet, peace and blessings of Allah be upon him, said:

"The case of a person who observes the limits set by Allah as compared to the one who breaks these limits is like that of a people who cast lots about reserving places in a boat. Some of them are alloted the upper deck while others get the lower. When those on the lower deck need water they have to pass by those who are above them. They suggest, 'If we make a hole in our part of the ship we will not disturb those above us.' If those on the upper deck let them do as they intend, all of them will be destroyed, while if they stop them, all of them will remain safe."

(Bukhari)

Inviting people to Allah

٤٤ - عَنْ سَهْلِ بْنِ سَعْدٍ رضى الله عنه اَنَّ النَّبِيَّ ﷺ قَالَ لِعَلِيٍّ
رضى الله عنه : فَوَاللهِ لَاَنْ يَهْدِىَ اللهُ بِكَ رَجُلاً وَاحِـدًا
خَيْرٌ لَكَ مِنْ حُمْرِ النَّعَم ـ

« مسلم كتاب الفضائل باب فضائل على بن ابى طالب و
بخارى كتاب الجهاد »

44. Sahl bin Sa'd, God be pleased with him, narrates that the
Holy Prophet, peace and blessings of Allah be upon him, said to
Ali, God be pleased with him, "By Allah! If Allah helps you to
guide a single person to the truth, it is better for you than (the most
precious) red camels." *(Muslim)*

٤٥ - عَنْ اَبِى هُرَيْرَةَ رضى الله عنه اَنَّ رَسُوْلَ اللهِ ﷺ قَالَ : مَنْ
دَعَـا اِلَى هُدًى كَانَ لَهُ مِنَ الاَجْرِ مِثْـلُ اُجُوْرِ مَنْ تَبِعَهُ
لَايَنْقُصُ ذَلِكَ مِنْ اُجُوْرِهِمْ شَيْئًا ـ وَمَنْ دَعَا اِلَى ضَلَالَةٍ
كَانَ عَلَيْهِ مِنَ الاِثْمِ مِثْلُ اثَامِ مَنْ تَبِعَهُ لَايَنْقُصُ ذَلِكَ مِنْ
اثَامِهِمْ شَيْئًا ـ

« مسلم كتاب العلم باب من سن حسنة او سيئة »

45. Abu Hurairah, God be pleased with him, narrates that the
Holy Prophet, peace and blessings of Allah be upon him, said:

'A person who invites people to the truth gets a reward equal
to the reward of all those who accept the truth (at his invitation),
while nothing will be subtracted from their rewards. Likewise a
person who entices others to sin carries the burden of all the sins
committed at his inducement, while nothing will be subtracted
from the punishment of those who commit the sins." *(Muslim)*

٤٦ - عَنْ اَنَسٍ رضى الله عنه عَنِ النَّبِىِّ ﷺ قَالَ : يَسِّرُوْا وَلَا
تُعَسِّرُوْا وَ بَشِّرُوْا وَلَا تُنَفِّرُوْا ـ

« مسلم كتاب الجهاد باب فى الامر بالتيسير وترك التنفير »

46.

Anas, God be pleased with him, narrates that the Holy Prophet, peace and blessings of Allah be upon him, said:

"Make religion easy for others to follow; do not make it difficult. Similarly, present religion in a pleasing manner; do not make it repulsive to others."   *(Muslim)*

Obligations and Prohibitions

٤٧ - عَنْ اَبِىْ ثَعْلَبَةَ الْخُشَنِىِّ جُرْثُوْمٍ بْنِ نَاشِرٍ رضى الله عنه عَنْ
رَسُوْلِ الله ﷺ قَالَ: اِنَّ اللهَ تَعَالَىْ فَرَضَ فَرَائِضَ فَلَا
تُضَيِّعُوْهَا ، وَحَدَّ حُدُوْدًا فَلَاتَعْتَدُوْهَا ، وَحَرَّمَ اَشْيَاءَ فَلَا
تَنْتَهِكُوْهَا وَسَكَتَ عَنْ اَشْيَاءَ رَحْمَةً لَكُمْ غَيْرَ نِسْيَانٍ فَلَا
تَبْحَثُوْا عَنْهَا -

« دارقطنى »

47. Abi Tha'labatal Khushaniyi Jurthoom bin Nashir, God be pleased with him, narrates that the Holy Prophet, peace and blessings of Allah be upon him, said:

"Allah The Almighty has laid down certain obligations: Do not disregard them. He has set certain limits: do not transgress them. He has forbidden certain things: Do not go near them. He has kept silent about some other things, out of kindness to you, not because of forgetfulness: so do not make unnecessary inquiries regarding them." *(Dar Qutni)*

٤٨ - عَنِ النُّعْمَانِ بْنِ بَشِيرٍ رضى الله عنه قَالَ: سَمِعْتُ رَسُوْلَ
الله ﷺ يَقُوْلُ: اِنَّ الْحَلَالَ بَيِّنٌ وَاِنَّ الْحَرَامَ بَيِّنٌ وَبَيْنَهُمَا
مُشْتَبِهَاتٌ لَا يَعْلَمُهُنَّ كَثِيْرٌ مِنَ النَّاسِ ، فَمَنِ اتَّقَى
الشُّبُهَاتِ اسْتَبْرَأَ لِدِيْنِهِ وَعِرْضِهِ ، وَمَنْ وَقَعَ فِى الشُّبُهَاتِ
وَقَعَ فِى الْحَرَامِ كَالرَّاعِىْ يَرْعَى حَوْلَ الْحِمَى يُوْشِكُ اَنْ
يَرْتَعَ فِيْهِ ، اَلَا وَاِنَّ لِكُلِّ مَلِكٍ حِمًى ، اَلَا وَاِنَّ حِمَى الله
مَحَارِمُهُ ، اَلَا وَاِنَّ فِى الْجَسَدِ مُضْغَةً اِذَا صَلَحَتْ صَلَحَ
الْجَسَدُ كُلُّهُ ، وَاِذَا فَسَدَتْ فَسَدَ الْجَسَدُ كُلُّهُ: اَلَا وَهِىَ
الْقَلْبُ - « مسلم كتاب البيوع باب اخذالحلال »

36

48. No'maan bin Basheer, God be pleased with him, said that he heard the Holy Prophet, peace and blessings of Allah be upon him, say:

"It has been made clear what is lawful and what is forbidden. In between the two there are certain things undefined: most people do not know which category they belong to. Whoever keeps away from them safeguards his faith and his honour. Whoever steps into the doubtful is likely to have stepped into the forbidden area. He is like a shepherd who lets his flock graze around a forbidden area, while there is every danger that the flock may stray into it. Remember that every sovereign has a forbidden area. The forbidden area of Allah comprises the things He has prohibited. Beware! There is an organ in the body as long as it remains healthy, the entire body remains healthy. The moment it becomes diseased, the entire body will become diseased. Remember that this organ is the heart." *(Muslim)*

Marriage

٤٩ - عَنْ أَبِىْ هُرَيْرَةَ رضى الله عنه عَنِ النَّبِىِّ ﷺ قَالَ: تُنْكَحُ
الْمَرْأَةُ لِأَرْبَعٍ لِمَالِهَا وَحَسَبِهَا وَلِجَمَالِهَا وَلِدِيْنِهَا ـ فَاظْفُرْ بِذَاتِ
الدِّيْنِ تَرِبَتْ يَدَاكَ ـ

« بخارى كتاب النكاح باب الاكفاء فى الدين »

49. Abu Hurairah, God be pleased with him, narrates that the Holy Prophet, peace and blessings of Allah be upon him, said:

"Usually one marries a woman for four reasons: For her wealth, for her family, for her beauty or for her righteousness. Give preference to the one who is righteous. May you remain humble." *(Bukhari)*

٥٠ - عَنْ أَبِىْ هُرَيْرَةَ رضى الله عنه اَنَّهُ كَانَ يَقُوْلُ: شَرُّالطَّعَامِ
طَعَامُ الْوَلِيْمَةِ يُدْعَى لَهَا الْاَغْنِيَاءُ وَيُتْرَكُ الْفُقَرَاءُ، وَمَنْ لَمْ
يُجِبِ الدَّعْوَةَ فَقَدْ عَصَى اللهَ وَرَسُوْلَهُ ـ

« مسلم كتاب النكاح باب الامر باجابة الداعى الى دعوة »

50. Abu Hurairah, God be pleased with him, relates that the Holy Prophet, peace and blessings of Allah be upon him, said:

"The worst marriage feast is the one in which only the rich are invited and the poor are left out. He who is invited (by a humble person) and refuses to accept the invitation (out of haughtiness) is disobedient to Allah and His Messenger." *(Muslim)*

١٥ ـ عَنِ ابْنِ عُمَـرَ رضى الله عنـه اَنَّ النَّبِيَّ ﷺ قَالَ : اَبْغَضُ
الْحَلَالِ اِلَى اللهِ عَزَّوَجَلَّ الطَّلَاقُ ـ

« ابو داود كتاب الطلاق باب فى كراهية الطلاق »

51. Ibn Omar, God be pleased with him, relates that the Holy
Prophet, peace and blessings of Allah be upon him, said:
'The most disliked of all the lawful things in the sight of Allah,
The Almighty, is divorce." *(Abu Dawood)*

٢٥ ـ عَنْ عَائِشَةَ قَالَتْ قَالَ رَسُولُ اللهِ صَلَّى اللّهُ عَلَيْهِ وَسَلَّمَ :
خَيْرُكُمْ خَيْرُكُمْ لِاهْلِهِ وَأَنَا خَيْرُكُمْ لِاهْلِيْ ـ

« ابو داؤد »

52. Ayesha, God be pleased with her, relates that the Holy
Prophet, peace and blessings of Allah be upon him, said:
"The best among you is the one who is best to his family and I
am the best of those who are good to their families."

(Abu Dawood)

Good Conduct

٥٣ - عَنْ جَابِرٍ رضى الله عنه اَنَّ رَسُوْلَ اللهِ ﷺ قَالَ: اِنَّ مِنْ
اَحَبِّكُمْ اِلَيَّ وَاَقْـرَبِكُمْ مِنِّيْ مَجْلِسًا يَوْمَ الْقِيَامَةِ اُحَاسِنُكُمْ
اَخْـلَاقًا وَاِنَّ مِنْ اَبْغَضِكُمْ اِلَيَّ وَاَبْعَدكُمْ مِّنِّيْ يَوْمَ الْقِيَامَةِ
الثَّرْثَارُوْنَ وَالْمُتَشَدِّقُوْنَ وَالْمُتَفَيْهِقُوْنَ ! قَالُوْا: يَارَسُوْلَ اللهِ
قَدْ عَلِمْنَا الثَّرْثَارُوْنَ وَالْمُتَشَدِّقُوْنَ فَمَا الْمُتَفَيْهِقُوْنَ ؟ قَالَ:
الْمُتَكَبِّرُوْنَ ـ

« ترمذى كتاب البروالصلة باب فى معالى الاخلاق »

53. Jaabir, God be pleased with him, narrates that the Holy
Prophet, peace and blessings of Allah be upon him, said:

"The one dearest to me and the one nearest to me on the Day
of Judgment, will be the one who is most well mannered. The
most loathsome from among you and furthest removed from me
on the Day of Judgment will be the boastful, the braggarts and the
al *mutafaihiqoon*." The Companions enquired, 'We know the
ones who are boastful and those who brag, but who are the
mutafaihiqoon?' The Holy Prophet answered, 'They are those
who are arrogant and spiteful."   *(Tirmidhi)*

٥٤ - عَنْ اَبِىْ هُرَيْرَةَ رضى الله عنه قَالَ قَالَ رَسُوْلُ اللهِ ﷺ: اِنَّمَا
بُعِثْتُ لِاُتَمِّمَ مَكَارِمَ الْاَخْلَاقِ ـ

« السنن الكبرى كتاب الشهادة باب بيان مكارم الاخلاق »

54. Abu Hurairah, God be pleased with him, narrates that the
Holy Prophet, peace and blessings of Allah be upon him, said:
'I have been sent to perfect the best of morals."

(Al Sunan al Kubra)

عَنْ أَبِى هُرَيْرَةَ رضى الله عنه عَنِ النَّبِيِّ ﷺ قَالَ : مَنْ نَفَّسَ
عَنْ مُؤْمِنٍ كُرْبَةً مِّنْ كُرَبِ الدُّنْيَا نَفَّسَ اللهُ عَنْهُ كُرْبَةً مِّنْ
كُرَبِ يَوْمِ الْقِيَامَةِ وَمَنْ يَّسَّرَ عَلَى مُعْسِرٍ يَسَّرَ اللهُ عَلَيْهِ فِى
الدُّنْيَا وَ الْاٰخِرَةِ وَمَنْ سَتَرَ مُسْلِمًا سَتَرَهُ اللهُ فِى الدُّنْيَا وَالْاٰخِرَةِ
وَاللهُ فِىْ عَوْنِ الْعَبْدِ مَاكَانَ الْعَبْدُ فِىْ عَوْنِ أَخِيْهِ ، وَمَنْ سَلَكَ
طَرِيْقًا يَّلْتَمِسُ فِيْهِ عِلْمًا سَهَّلَ اللهُ بِهِ طَرِيْقًا اِلَى الْجَنَّةِ ، وَمَا
اجْتَمَعَ قَوْمٌ فِىْ بَيْتٍ مِّنْ بُيُوْتِ اللهِ تَعَالَى يَتْلُوْنَ كِتَابَ اللهِ
وَيَتَدَارَسُوْنَهُ بَيْنَهُمْ اِلَّا نَزَلَتْ عَلَيْهِمُ السَّكِيْنَةُ وَغَشِيَتْهُمُ
الرَّحْمَةُ وَحَفَّتْهُمُ الْمَلَائِكَةُ وَذَكَرَهُمُ اللهُ فِيْمَنْ عِنْدَهُ ، وَمَنْ
بَطَّأَبِهِ عَمَلُهُ لَمْ يُسْرِعْ بِهِ نَسَبُهُ ـ

«مسلم كتاب الذكر باب فضل الاجتماع على تلاوة القرآن
و على الذكر »

55. Abu Hurairah, God be pleased with him, relates that the Holy Prophet, peace and blessings of Allah be upon him, stated:

"Whoever relieves a believer of his worries in this world will have his afflictions removed by Allah on the Day of Judgment. Whoever is lenient to someone whose means of sustenance have been straitened, Allah will be lenient to him in this world and the next. Whoever covers the weakness of a Muslim, Allah will provide him cover in this world and in the world to come. Allah always stands by the side of the one who is helpful to his brother. Whoever treads a path in pursuit of knowledge, Allah will facilitate thereby his way to Paradise. Those who gather in any of the Houses of Allah to recite the Book of Allah and teach each other, are certainly blessed with tranquility; they are covered by His mercy and are surrounded by the angels. Allah mentions them to those who are closest to Him. The one who is left behind because of his deeds, will not have his cause advanced because of the good name of his family." *(Muslim)*

٥٦ - عَنْ اَبِىْ هُرَيْرَةَ قَالَ قَالَ رَسُوْلُ اللهِ ﷺ اِنَّ اللهَ عَزَّوَجَلَّ
يَقُوْلُ يَوْمَ الْقِيَامَةِ : يَا ابْنَ اٰدَمَ مَرِضْتُ فَلَمْ تَعُدْنِىْ قَالَ :
يَارَبِّ كَيْفَ اَعُوْدُكَ وَاَنْتَ رَبُّ الْعَالَمِيْنَ قَالَ : أَمَا عَلِمْتَ اَنَّ
عَبْدِىْ فُلَانًا مَرِضَ فَلَمْ تَعُدْهُ أَمَا عَلِمْتَ اَنَّكَ لَوْعُدْتَّهُ
لَوَجَدْتَنِىْ عِنْـدَهُ ، يَا ابْنَ اٰدَمَ اسْتَطْعَمْتُكَ فَلَمْ تُطْعِمْنِى
قَالَ : يَارَبِّ وَكَيْفَ أُطْعِمُكَ وَأَنْتَ رَبُّ الْعَالَمِيْنَ قَالَ : أَمَا
عَلِمْتَ اَنَّهُ اسْتَطْعَمَكَ عَبْدِىْ فُلَانٌ فَلَمْ تُطْعِمْهُ أَمَاعَلِمْتَ
أَنَّـكَ لَوْ أَطْعَمْتَـهُ لَوَجَدْتَّ ذٰلِكَ عِنْـدِىْ ـ يَا ابْنَ اٰدَمَ
اسْتَسْقَيْتُكَ فَلَمْ تَسْقِنِىْ ، قَالَ : يَارَبِّ كَيْفَ اَسْقِيْكَ وَأَنْتَ
رَبُّ الْعَالَمِيْنَ قَالَ اسْتَسْقَاكَ عَبْدِىْ فُلَانٌ فَلَمْ تَسْقِهِ أَمَا اِنَّكَ
لَوْ سَقَيْتَهُ وَجَدْتَّ ذٰلِكَ عِنْدِىْ ـ

«مسلم كتاب البروالصلة باب فضل عيادة المريض»

56. Abu Hurairah, God be pleased with him, relates that the Holy Prophet, peace and blessings of Allah be upon him, said:

"On the Day of Judgment, Allah The Almighty will say, '0 son of Adam! I was ill, why did you not enquire after Me when I was ill?' He will respond, 'How could I enquire after your health while you are the Lord of the universe?' Allah will reply, 'Were you not aware that a servant of Mine fell ill and you failed to inquire after him? Had you done so, you would have found Me by his side. 0 son of Adam! I begged you for food and you did not feed me.' He will respond, '0 my Lord, how could I have fed you, while you are the Lord of the universe?' Allah will say, 'Did you not realize that when a servant of Mine asked you for food and you refused to oblige him, if you had fed him I would have appreciated it as if you had done it to Me. 0 son of Adam! I asked thee to quench My thirst, and you refused to do so.' He will say, ' How could I quench your thirst, while You are the Lord of the universe?' Allah will say, When a servant of Mine asked you to quench his thirst and you did not respond, had you done so I would have appreciated it as if you had done it to Me." *(Muslim)*

٥٧ ـ قَالَ النَّبِيُّ ﷺ اِنَّكُمْ لَنْ تَسَعُوْا النَّاسَ بِاَمْوَالِكُمْ فَسَعُوْهُمْ بِبَسْطِ الْوَجْهِ وَحُسْنِ الْخُلُقِ ـ

« رساله قشيريه ، باب الخلق ص ١٢١ »

57. The Holy Prophet, peace and blessings of Allah be upon him, said:

"You can never enrich people with your money alone; so help them cheerfully and with good grace." *(Risalah Qushariyyah)*

The Islamic Society

٥٨ - عَنْ اَنَسٍ رضى الله عنـه عَنِ النَّبِيَّ ﷺ قَالَ: لَا يُؤْمِنُ اَحَدُكُمْ حَتَّى يُحِبَّ لِاَخِيهِ مَايُحِبُّ لِنَفْسِهِ ـ

«بخـارى كتـاب الايمان باب من الايمان ان يحب لاخيه مايحب لنفسه »

58. Anas, God be pleased with him, relates that the Holy Prophet, peace and blessings of Allah be upon him, said:

"None of you is a true believer unless he likes for others that which he likes for himself." *(Bukhari)*

٥٩ - عَنْ اَبِىْ هُرَيْرَةَ قَالَ قَالَ رَسُوْلُ اللهِ ﷺ يَا اَبَاهُرَيْرَةَ كُنْ وَرِعًا تَكُنْ اَعْبَدَ النَّاسِ وَكُنْ قَنِعًا تَكُنْ اَشْكَرَ النَّاسِ وَاَحِبَّ لِلنَّاسِ مَاتُحِبُّ لِنَفْسِكَ تَكُنْ مُؤْمِنًا وَاَحْسِنْ جِوَارَ مَنْ جَاوَرَكَ تَكُنْ مُسْلِمًا وَاَقِلَّ الضَّحْكَ فَاِنَّ كَثْرَةَ الضَّحْكِ تُمِيْتُ الْقَلْبَ ـ

«ابن ماجه كتاب الزهد باب الورع والتقوى »

59. Abu Hurairah, God be pleased with him, states that the Holy Prophet, peace and blessings of Allah be upon him, said:

"O Abu Hurairah, be righteous and you will be the best of worshippers. Be content, so that you can be the best of those who are grateful. Choose for others what you like for yourself, then you will become a (true) believer. Treat your neighbour in the best of manners then you will be worthy of being a Muslim. Do not laugh excessively, because excessive laughter causes the heart to die." *(Ibn Maajah)*

٦٠ - عَنْ أَبِي يُوْسُفَ عَبْدِالله بْنِ سَلَامٍ رضى الله عنه قَالَ:
سَمِعْتُ رَسُـوْلَ الله ﷺ يَقُـوْلُ: يَاأَيُّـهَا النَّـاسُ أَفْشُـوا
السَّلَامَ ، وَأَطْعِمُوا الطَّعَامَ ، وَ صِلُوا الأَرْحَامَ ، وَصَلُّوا
وَالنَّاسُ نِيَامٌ ، تَدْخُلُوا الْجَنَّةَ بِسَلَامٍ ۔

«ترمذى ابواب صفة القيٰمة»

60. Abu Yusuf Abdullah bin Salaam, God be pleased with him, relates: "I heard the Holy Prophet, peace and blessings of Allah be upon him, say:

'0 people! Say *Assalamo Alaikum*! Feed others! Be mindful of your obligations towards relatives! Worship (Allah) while others are asleep! Do this, and you will enter Paradise in peace."

(Tirmidhi)

٦١ - عَنِ ابْنِ مَسْعُوْدٍ رضى الله عنه أَنَّ رَسُوْلَ الله ﷺ قَالَ: اذَا
كُنْتُمْ ثَلَاثَةً فَلَا يَتَنَاجَى اثْنَانِ دُوْنَ الاخَرِ حَتَّى تَخْتَلِطُوْا
بِالنَّاسِ مِنْ أَجْلِ أَنَّ ذٰلِكَ يُحْزِنُهُ ۔

«مسلم كتاب السـلام باب تحريم منـاجاة الاثنين دون
الثالث بغير رضاه»

61. Ibn Mas'ood, God be pleased with him, relates that the Holy Prophet, peace and blessings of Allah be upon him, said:

"When there are three of you together, two of you should not talk to each other excluding the third, as it will hurt him, unless you are joined by others." *(Muslim)*

٦٢- عَنْ اَبِىْ هُرَيْرَةَ رضى الله عنه قَالَ: كَانَ رَسُوْلُ الله ﷺ
اِذَاعَطَسَ وَضَعَ يَدَهُ اَوْثَوْبَهُ عَلَىٰ فِيْهِ وَخَفَضَ اَوْ غَضَّ بِهَا
صَوْتَهُ شَكَّ الرَّاوِىْ ـ

« ترمذى كتاب الاستيذان باب فى خفض الصوت و تخمير

الوجه »

62. Abu Hurairah, God be pleased with him, relates:

"It was the practice of the Holy Prophet, peace and blessings of
Allah be upon him, that when he sneezed he would cover his
mouth with his hand or a piece of cloth, thus subduing it." Maybe
the narrator used another word instead of 'subduing' meaning the
same."   (Tirmidhi)

Being Grateful to People

٦٣ - عَنْ اَبِىْ هُرَيْرَةَ قَالَ قَالَ رَسُوْلُ اللهِ ﷺ مَنْ لَّايَشْكُرِ النَّاسَ
لَايَشْكُرِ اللهَ ۔

« ترمذى باب ماجاء فى الشكر لمن احسن اليك »

63. Abu Hurairah, God be pleased with him, relates that the Holy Prophet, peace and blessings of Allah be upon him, said: "He who is not grateful to people is not grateful to Allah."

(Tirmidhi)

The Good Treatment of Parents

٦٤ ـ   عَنْ اَبِىْ هُرَيْرَةَ رضى الله عنه قَالَ: جَاءَ رَجُلٌ اِلَى رَسُوْلِ
اللهِ ﷺ فَقَـالَ: يَارَسُوْلَ اللهِ مَنْ اَحَقُّ النَّاسِ بِحُسْنِ
صَحَابَتِىْ؟ قَالَ: اُمُّكَ قَالَ ثُمَّ مَنْ؟ قَالَ اُمُّكَ قَالَ: ثُمَّ مَنْ
؟ قَالَ: اُمُّكَ قَالَ: ثُمَّ مَنْ؟ قَالَ: اَبُوْكَ ـ وَفِىْ رِوَايَةٍ
يَارَسُوْلَ اللهِ مَنْ اَحَقُّ بِحُسْنِ الصُّحْبَةِ؟ قَالَ اُمُّكَ ثُمَّ اُمُّكَ
ثُمَّ اُمُّكَ ثُمَّ اَبَاكَ ثُمَّ اَدْنَاكَ اَدْنَاكَ ـ

« بخارى كتاب الادب باب من احق الناس بحسن
الصحبة »

64. Abu Hurairah, God be pleased with him, relates:

"A man approached the Holy Prophet, peace and blessings of Allah be upon him, and enquired, '0 Messenger of Allah! Of all people, with whom should I have the best relationship?' He replied, 'Your mother.' The man enquired a second time, And then who?' The Holy Prophet replied, Your mother again.' The man asked a third time, 'Who then?' 'Again your mother' was the reply. The man asked once more, 'Then who?' The Holy Prophet, peace and blessings of Allah be upon him, replied, 'Your father'. According to another version, the questioner asked, '0 Prophet of Allah! Who deserves the best of treatment?" The Holy Prophet replied, 'Your mother, then your mother, then your mother, then your father and then the next of kin." *(Bukhari)*

عَنْ اَبِىْ هُرَيْرَةَ رضى الله عنه عَن النَّبِىِّ ﷺ قَالَ : رَغِمَ — ٦٥
اَنْفُ ثُمَّ رَغِمَ اَنْفُ ثُمَّ رَغِمَ اَنْفُ مَنْ اَدْرَكَ اَبَوَيْهِ عِنْدَ
الْكِبَرِ اَحَدَهُمَا اَوْ كِلَيْهِمَا فَلَمْ يَدْخُل الْجَنَّةَ ۔

« مسلم كتاب البر والصلة باب رغم انف من ادرك ابويه »

65. Abu Hurairah, God be pleased with him, relates that the
Holy Prophet, peace and blessings of Allah be upon him, said:

"Poorly is the person, poorly is the person, again, poorly is the
person, the one who lives long enough to witness the old age of
his parents, yet fails to earn Paradise (by serving them)." *(Muslim)*

Good Neighbourliness

عَن ابْنِ عُمَرَ وَ عَائِشَةَ رضى الله عنهما قَالَا : قَالَ رَسُوْلُ اللهِ ٦٦ـ

ﷺ : مَازَالَ جِبْرِيْلُ يُوْصِيْنِيْ بِالْجَارِ حَتَّى ظَنَنْتُ أَنَّهُ

سَيُوَرِّثُهُ ـ

« بخارى كتاب الادب باب الوصايا بالجار »

66. Ibn 'Umar and Ayesha, God be pleased with them, relate that the Holy Prophet, peace and blessings of Allah be upon him, said:

"Gabriel kept exhorting me about the rights of neighbours until I was inclined to believe that he would give them even the right of inheritance." *(Bukhari)*

عَنْ أَبِىْ هُرَيْرَةَ رضى الله عنه أَنَّ رَسُوْلَ اللهِ ﷺ قَالَ : مَنْ ٦٧ـ

كَانَ يُؤْمِنُ بِاللهِ وَالْيَوْمِ الْاٰخِرِ فَلَايُؤْذِ جَارَهُ ، وَمَنْ كَانَ

يُؤْمِنُ بِاللهِ وَالْيَوْمِ الْاٰخِرِ فَلْيُكْرِمْ ضَيْفَهُ ، وَمَنْ كَانَ يُؤْمِنُ

بِاللهِ وَالْيَوْمِ الْاٰخِرِ فَلْيَقُلْ خَيْرًا اَوْلِيَسْكُتْ ـ

« بخارى كتاب الادب باب من كان يومن بالله واليوم

الاٰخر »

67. Abu Hurairah, God be pleased with him, relates that the Holy Prophet, peace and blessings of Allah be upon him, said:

"Whoever believes in Allah and the Day of Judgement should not put his neighbour to inconvenience. Whoever believes in Allah and the Day of Judgement should treat his guests with respect. Whoever believes in Allah and the Day of Judgement should only say that which is good or else remain quiet." *(Bukhari)*

عَنْ أَبِىْ هُرَيْرَةَ رضى الله عنه اَنَّ النَّبِيَّ ﷺ قَالَ : وَاللهِ لَا

يُؤْمِنُ وَاللهِ لَاَيُؤْمِنُ وَاللهِ لَاَيُؤْمِنُ ! قِيْلَ : مَنْ يَارَسُوْلَ اللهِ ؟

قَالَ : اَلَّذِىْ لَاَيَأْمَنُ جَارُهُ بَوَائِقَهُ ۔

« بخارى كتاب الادب باب اثم من لايأمن جاره بوائقه »

68. Abu Hurairah, God be pleased with him, relates that the Holy Prophet, peace and blessings of Allah be upon him, said:

"I testify in the name of God: He does not believe. I testify in the name of God: He does not believe. I testify in the name of God: He does not believe.' The Holy Prophet was asked, 'Who does not believe?' He replied, 'He whose neighbour is not safe from his mischief." *(Bukhari)*

Kindness Towards the Weak

٦٩ ـ   عَنْ أَبِىْ هُرَيْرَةَ رضى الله عنه قَالَ : قَالَ رَسُوْلُ اللهِ ﷺ :
رُبَّ أَشْعَثَ أَغْبَرَ مَدْفُوْعٍ بِالأَبْوَابِ لَوْأَقْسَمَ عَلَى اللهِ
لَأَبَرَّهُ ـ

« مسلم كتاب الجنة باب النار يدخلها الجبارون »

69. Abu Hurairah, God be pleased with him, relates that the Holy Prophet, peace and blessings of Allah be upon him, said:

"There are some people who look shabby, with dishevelled, dusty hair. Doors are closed upon them in disdain. Yet (they have a station with their God so that) when they swear by Him, He makes their word come true."   *(Muslim)*

٧٠ ـ   عَنْ أَبِى الدَّرْدَاءِ رضى الله عنه قَالَ : سَمِعْتُ رَسُوْلَ اللهِ
ﷺ يَقُوْلُ ابْغُوْنِىْ فِىْ ضُعَفَائِكُمْ فَاِنَّمَا تُرْزَقُوْنَ وَتُنْصَرُوْنَ
بِضُعَفَائِكُمْ ـ

« ترمذى كتاب الجهاد باب ماجاء فى الاستفتاح بصعاليك المسلمين »

70. Abu Darda, God be pleased with him, relates that he heard the Holy Prophet, peace and blessings of Allah be upon him, say:

"Seek me in the midst of the weak and the poor; verily you are sustained and supported by their labour."   *(Tirmidhi)*

Forgiveness

٧١ ـ عَنْ مُعَاذِ بْنِ اَنَسٍ رضى الله عنه عَنْ رَسُوْلِ اللهِ ﷺ اَنَّهُ
قَالَ : اَفْضَلُ الْفَضَائِلِ اَنْ تَصِلَ مَنْ قَطَعَكَ وَ تُعْطِىَ مَنْ
مَنَعَكَ وَ تَصْفَحَ عَمَّنْ شَتَمَكَ ـ

« مسند احمد ص ٣/٤٣٨ »

71. Mu'az bin Anas, God be pleased with him, related that the
Holy Prophet, peace and blessings of Allah be upon him, said:

"The height of excellence is that you should strengthen the ties
of relationship with the one who severs them and be generous to
the one who is miserly to you and be forgiving to the one who
abuses you."   *(Musnad Ahmad)*

٧٢ ـ عَنْ اَبِىْ هُرَيْــرَةَ رضى الله عنه عَنِ النَّبِىِّ ﷺ قَالَ : مَا
نَقَصَتْ صَدَقَةٌ مِنْ مَالٍ وَلاَ عَفَا رَجُلٌ عَنْ مَظْلِمَةٍ اِلاَّ زَادَهُ
اللهُ عِزًّا وَلاَ تَوَاضَعَ ـ

« مسند احمد ص ٢/٢٣٥ ، ٢/٤٣٨ »

72. Abu Hurairah, God be pleased with him, relates that the
Holy Prophet, peace and blessings of Allah be upon him, said:

Giving of alms does not diminish one's wealth. Allah bestows
honour on, and raises the status of, the one who forgives any
excess committed against him and who does not treat the
transgressor with haughtiness."   *(Musnad Ahmad)*

Table Manners

٧٣ ـ عَنْ عَائِشَةَ رضى الله عنها قَالَتْ : قَالَ رَسُوْلُ الله ﷺ : اذَا
اَكَلَ اَحَدُكُمْ فَلْيَذْكُرْ اِسْمَ الله تَعَالَى فَانْ نَسِيَ اَنْ يَّذكُرَ اِسْمَ
الله تَعَالَى فِيْ اَوَّلِهِ فَلْيَقُلْ : بِسْمِ الله اَوَّلَهُ وَاخِرَهُ ـ
« ترمذى كتاب الاطعمة باب ماجاء فى التسمية على الطعام »

73. Ayesha, God be pleased with her, relates that the Holy
Prophet, peace and blessings of Allah be upon him, said:

"Whenever one of you begins to eat, he should first say 'In the
name of Allah The Exalted.' If he forgets to do so in the beginning,
then, at the end of the meal, he should say, *'Bismillahe awwalahu
wa akherahu.'* 'In the name of Allah, do I begin and end."

(Tirmidhi)

٧٤ ـ عَنْ اَبِىْ سَعِيْدٍ قَالَ كَانَ النَّبِىُّ ﷺ اذَا اَكَلَ اَوْ شَرِبَ قَالَ
اَلْحَمْدُ لِلَّهِ الَّذِىْ اَطْعَمَنَا وَسَقَانَا وَجَعَلَنَا مُسْلِمِيْنَ ـ
« ترمذى كتاب الدعوات باب مايقول اذا فرغ من
الطعام »

74, Abu Sa'eed, God be pleased with him, narrates that
whenever the Holy Prophet, peace and blessings of Allah be upon
him, would eat or drink, he would say:

"All praise belongs to Allah who provided us with food and drink
and made us Muslims.' *(Tirmidhi)*

Matters of Dress

٧٥ ـ عَنْ حُذَيْفَةَ رضى الله عنـه قَالَ : اِنَّ النَّبِيَّ ﷺ نَهَانَا عَنِ
الْحَرِيرِ وَ الدِّيْبَاجِ وَالشُّرْبِ فِى اٰنِيَةِ الذَّهَبِ وَالْفِضَّةِ وَ قَالَ :
هِىَ لَهُمْ فِى الدُّنْيَا وَهِىَ لَكُمْ فِى الْاٰخِرَةِ ـ
«مسلم كتـاب اللبـاس والزينة باب تحريم استعمال اناء
الذهب والفضة »

75. Hudhaifa, God be pleased with him, relates:

"The Holy Prophet, peace and blessings of Allah be upon him,
forbade us to wear silk and brocade. He also forbade us to eat or
drink out of gold or silver vessels, saying that they are for them (the
non believers) in this world, and for you in the Hereafter." *(Muslim)*

٧٦ ـ عَنْ اَبِىْ سَعِيْدِ الْخُدْرِىِّ رضى الله عنه قَالَ : كَانَ رَسُوْلُ اللهِ
ﷺ اِذَا اسْتَجَدَّ ثَوْبًا سَمَّاهُ بِاسْمِهِ عَمَامَةً ، اَوْقَمِيْصًا ، اَوْ
رِدَاءً ـ يَقُوْلُ اللَّهُمَّ لَكَ الْحَمْدُ اَنْتَ كَسَوْتَنِيْهِ وَاَسْاَلُكَ خَيْرَهُ
وَخَيْرَمَا صُنِعَ لَهُ ، وَاَعُوْذُ بِكَ مِنْ شَرِّهِ وَشَرِّمَا صُنِعَ لَهُ ـ
«ترمذى كتاب اللباس باب مايقول اذا لبس ثوبا جديدا »

76. Abu Sa'eed al Khudri, God be pleased with him narrates
that when the Holy Prophet, peace and blessings of Allah be upon
him, wore a new dress, he would first mention what type of dress
it was, for instance, turban, shirt or cloak, and then he would
supplicate as follows:

"Allah, Thine is the praise. Thou hast given this to me to wear.
I beg of Thee the benefit that it contains, and beg Thee to help me
to put it to the best use for which it was made; also I seek Thy
protection against whatever harm there may be in it and against
whatever harmful purpose it may have been made for." *(Tirmidhi)*

Cleanliness

٧٧ - عَنْ اَبِىْ مَالِكٍ الْاَشْعَرِيِّ رضى الله عنه قَالَ : قَالَ رَسُوْلُ
اللهِ ﷺ اَلطُّهُوْرُ شَطْرُ الْاِيْمَانِ -

« مسلم كتاب الطهارة باب فضل الوضوء »

77. Abu Musa al Ash'ari, God be pleased with him, relates that
the Holy Prophet, peace and blessings of Allah be upon him, said:
"Cleanliness is a requirement of faith."   *(Muslim)*

٧٨ - عَنْ عَائِشَةَ رضى الله عنها اَنَّ النَّبِىَّ ﷺ قَالَ : السِّوَاكُ
مَطْهَرَةٌ لِلْفَمِ مَرْضَاةٌ لِلرَّبِّ

« نسائى باب الترغيب فى السواك »

78. Ayesha, God be pleased with her, relates that the Holy
Prophet, peace and blessings of Allah be upon him, said:
"Brushing the teeth keeps the mouth clean and pleases Allah."
(Nasaai)

Envy

٧٩ -   عَنِ ابْنِ عُمَرَ رضى الله عنه قَالَ : قَالَ رَسُوْلُ اللهِ ﷺ :
لاَتَحَاسَدُوْا وَلاَ تَنَاجَشُوْا وَلاَ تَبَاغَضُوْا وَلاَ تَدَابَرُوْا وَلاَ يَبِعْ
بَعْضُكُمْ عَلَى بَيْعِ بَعْضٍ ، وَكُوْنُوْا عِبَادَ اللهِ اخْوَانًا ـ
اَلْمُسْلِمُ اَخُوالْمُسْلِمِ : لاَ يَظْلِمُهُ وَلاَ يَحْقِرُهُ ولاَيَخْذُلُهُ ـ
اَلتَّقْوَى هُهُنَا   وَيُشِيْرُ الَى صَدْرِه ثَلاَثَ مَرَاتٍ،بِحَسْبِ
امْرِىءٍ مِّنَ الشَّرِّ اَنْ يَحْقِرَ اَخَاهُ الْمُسْلِمَ ـ كُلُّ الْمُسْلِمِ عَلَى
الْمُسْلِمِ حَرَامٌ دَمُهُ وَمَالُهُ وَعِرْضُهُ ـ
«مسلم كتاب البروالصلة باب تحريم ظلم المسلم و
خذله »

79. Abdullah bin Omar, God be pleased with him, says that the
Holy Prophet, peace and blessings of Allah be upon him, stated:

"Do not be jealous of each other. Do not inflate prices. Do not
hate each other. Do not turn your back on each other. Do not
make an offer while two parties are engaged in bargaining. Be true
servants of God by becoming brothers to one another."

"Muslims are brothers to (other) Muslims. One should not
transgress against the other; he should not treat the other with
disdain, nor should he forsake him."

"Here dwells *taqwa* (the fear of God)" said the Holy Prophet
and he pointed to his chest three times. Then he said: 'It is enough
to ruin one to disdain one's brother Muslim. The blood, the
property and the honour of a Muslim is inviolable to another
Muslim." *(Muslim)*

٨٠- عَنْ اَبِىْ هُرَيْرَةَ رضى الله عنه اَنَّ النَّبِيَّ ﷺ قَالَ : اِيَّاكُمْ
وَالْحَسَدَ ؛ فَاِنَّ الْحَسَدَ يَاْكُلُ الْحَسَنَاتِ كَمَا تَاْكُلُ النَّارُ الْحَطَبَ
اَوْ قَالَ الْعُشْبَ ـ

«ابوداود كتاب الادب باب فى الحسد»

80. Abu Hurairah, God be pleased with him, relates that the
Holy Prophet, peace and blessings of Allah be upon him, said:

"Beware of the fire of jealousy, because it consumes good
deeds just as fire consumes wood and straw." *(Abu Dawood)*

Arrogance

٨١ ‑ عَنْ عَبْدِاللهِ بْنِ مَسْعُودٍ رضى الله عنه عَنِ النَّبِيِّ ﷺ قَالَ :
لَايَدْخُلُ الْجَنَّةَ مَنْ كَانَ فِيْ قَلْبِهِ مِثْقَالُ ذَرَّةٍ مِنْ كِبْرٍ فَقَالَ
رَجُلٌ : اِنَّ الرَّجُلَ يُحِبُّ اَنْ يَكُوْنَ ثَوْبُهُ حَسَنًا وَّ نَعْلُهُ حَسَنَةً
قَالَ : اِنَّ اللهَ جَمِيْلٌ يُحِبُّ الْجَمَالَ ، اَلْكِبْرُ بَطَرُالْحَقِّ وَغَمْطُ
النَّاسِ ‑

«مسلم كتاب الايمان تحريم الكبر وبيانه»

81. Abdullah bin Mas'ood, God be pleased with him, states
that the Holy Prophet, peace and blessings of Allah be upon him,
said:

"He who has a jot of arrogance in his heart will not enter
Paradise. Someone said, 'What about a person who likes to have
beautiful clothes and beautiful shoes?' The Prophet answered,
'Allah is Beauty and He loves beauty. (One cannot be called
arrogant if one beautifies oneself). Arrogance lies in the rejection
of the truth and in looking down upon people." *(Muslim)*

٨٢ ‑ عَنْ عَبْدِاللهِ رضى الله عنه قَالَ : قَالَ رَسُوْلُ اللهِ ﷺ عَلَيْكُمْ
بِالصِّدْقِ فَاِنَّ الصِّدْقَ يَهْدِىْ اِلَى الْبِرِّ وَاِنَّ الْبِرَّ يَهْدِىْ اِلَى
اْلجَنَّةِ وَمَايَزَالُ الـرَّجُلُ يَصْدُقُ وَيَتَحَرَّى الصِّدْقَ حَتَّى
يُكْتَبَ عِنْدَ اللهِ صِدِّيْقًا وَاِيَّاكُمْ وَالْكَذِبَ فَاِنَّ الْكَذِبَ يَهْدِىْ
اِلَى الْفُجُوْرِ وَاِنَّ الْفُجُوْرَ يَهْدِىْ اِلَى النَّارِ وَمَايَزَالُ الرَّجُلُ
يَكْذِبُ وَيَتَحَرَّى الْكَذِبَ حَتَّى يُكْتَبَ عِنْدَ اللهِ كَذَّابًا ‑

«مسلم كتـاب الـبـروالصلة بـاب قبـح الكـذب وحسن
الصدق وفضله»

59

82. Abdullah, God be pleased with him, narrates that the Holy Prophet, peace and blessings of Allah be upon him, said:

"You should adhere to truthfulness because it leads to virtue and virtue leads to Paradise. If a person speaks the truth and remains in pursuit of truth, a time comes when he is adjudged truthful by Allah. Beware of lying, because lying leads to vice and vice leads to Hell. If a person continues to tell lies and persists in doing so, a time comes when he is adjudged a liar of the first degree by Allah."   *(Muslim)*

٨٣ - عَنْ اَبِىْ بَكْرَةَ رضى الله عنه قَالَ : قَالَ رَسُوْلُ اللهِ ﷺ اَلَا اُنَبِّئُكُمْ بِاَكْبَرِ الْكَبَـائِرِ ؟ قُلْنَـا : بَلَى يَارَسُوْلَ اللهِ قَالَ : اَلْاِشْرَاكُ بِاللهِ ، وَ عُقُوْقُ الْوَالِدَيْنِ ، وَكَانَ مُتَّكَأً فَجَلَسَ فَقَالَ : اَلَا وَقَوْلَ الزُّوْرِ! فَمَازَالَ يُكَرِّرُهَا حَتَّى قُلْنَا : لَيْتَهُ سَكَتَ ،

«بخارى كتاب الادب باب عقوق الوالدين »

83. Abu Bakra, God be pleased with him, narrates that the Holy Prophet, peace and blessings of Allah be upon him, said:

"Should I not tell you about the worst of sins?"

We said, 'Please do, O Messenger of Allah.'

The Holy Prophet, peace and blessings of Allah be upon him, said: "Associating anyone with Allah and disobeying parents."

The Holy Prophet, peace and blessings of Allah be upon him, was reclining then he sat up and said, 'Beware of telling lies.' He kept on repeating it till we wished he would stop."

(Bukhari)

The Decline of Islam

٨٤- عَنْ عَبْدِاللهِ بْنِ عَمْرٍو رضى الله عنهما قَالَ قَالَ رَسُوْلُ اللهِ
ﷺ لَيَأْتِيَنَّ عَلَى أُمَّتِىْ مَا أَتَى عَلَى بَنِىْ إِسْرَائِيْلَ حَذْوَالنَّعْلِ
بِالنَّعْلِ حَتَّى اِنْ كَانَ مِنْهُم مَّنْ اَتَى اُمَّهُ عَلَانِيَةً لَكَانَ فِىْ اُمَّتِىْ
مَنْ يَّصْنَعُ ذٰلِكَ وَاِنَّ بَنِىْ اِسْرَائِيْلَ تَفَرَّقَتْ عَلَى اثْنَتَيْنِ
وَسَبْعِيْنَ مِلَّةً وَتَفْتَرِقُ اُمَّتِىْ عَلَى ثَلَاثٍ وَّسَبْعِيْنَ مِلَّةً كُلُّهُمْ فِى
النَّارِ اِلَّا مِلَّةً وَّاحِدَةً قَالُوْا : مَنْ هِىَ يَارَسُوْلَ اللهِ ؟ قَالَ :
مَاأَنَاعَلَيْهِ وَاَصْحَابِىْ ـ

« ترمذى كتاب الايمان باب افتراق هذه الامة »

84. Abdullah bin 'Amr, God be pleased with him, relates that the Holy Prophet, peace and blessings of Allah be upon him, said:

"Surely things will happen to my people as happened earlier to the Israelites. They will resemble each other like one shoe in a pair resembles the other to the extent that if anyone among the Israelites had openly committed adultery with his mother, there will be some who would do this in my *ummah* (people) as well. Verily, the Israelites were divided into 72 sects, but my people will be divided into 73 sects. All of them will be in the Fire except one.' The Companions asked, 'Who are they, O Messenger of Allah?' The Holy Prophet, peace and blessings of Allah be upon him, said: They are the people who will follow my practice and that of my companions." *(Tirmidhi)*

٨٥ ـ عَنْ عَلِيٍّ رضى الله عنه قَالَ قَالَ رَسُوْلُ اللهِ ﷺ يُوْشِكُ اَنْ يَأْتِيَ عَلَى النَّاسِ زَمَانٌ لَايَبْقَى مِنَ الْاِسْلَامِ اِلَّا اسْمُهُ وَلَايَبْقَى مِنَ الْقُرْانِ اِلَّا رَسْمُهُ مَسَاجِدُ هُمْ عَامِرَةٌ وَهِىَ خَرَابٌ مِنَ الْهُدَى عُلَمَآؤُهُمْ شَرُّمَنْ تَحْتَ اَدِيْمِ السَّمَآءِ مِنْ عِنْدِهِمْ تَخْرُجُ الْفِتْنَةُ وَفِيْهِمْ تَعُوْدُ ـ

«مشكوة كتاب العلم ،

85. Ali, God be pleased with him, relates that the Holy Prophet, peace and blessings of Allah be upon him, said:

"A time will come when nothing will remain of Islam except its name and nothing will remain of the Qur'an except its script. Mosques will be full of worshippers, but as far as righteousness is concerned they will be empty and deserted. Their *'ulama'* (religious scholars) will be the worst of creatures under the canopy of the heavens. Evil plots will originate from them and to them will they return." *(Mishkat)*

The Advent of Imam Mahdi

٨٦ - عَنْ أَبِى هُرَيْرَةَ رضى الله عنه قَالَ كُنَّاجُلُوْسًا عِنْدَ النَّبِىِّ ﷺ
إِذْ نَزَلَتْ عَلَيْهِ سُوْرَةُ الْجُمُعَةِ فَلَمَّا قَرَأَ وَاخَرِيْنَ مِنْهُمْ لَمَّا
يَلْحَقُوْا بِهِمْ قَالَ رَجُلٌ : مَنْ هؤُلَاءِ يَارَسُوْلَ اللهِ : فَلَمْ
يُرَاجِعْهُ النَّبِىُّ ﷺ حَتَّى سَأَلَهُ مَرَّةً أَوْ مَرَّتَيْنِ أَوْثَلَاثًا قَالَ
وَفِيْنَا سَلْمَانُ الْفَارِسِىُّ قَالَ فَوَضَعَ النَّبِىُّ ﷺ يَدَهُ عَلَى سَلْمَانَ
ثُمَّ قَالَ لَوْكَانَ الْاِيْمَانُ عِنْدَ الثُّرَيَّا لَنَالَهُ رِجَالٌ مِنْ هؤُلَاءِ ۔

« بخارى كتاب التفسير سورة جمعة ، مسلم ص ١٧٠ »

86. Abu Hurairah, God be pleased with him, narrates:

"When Sura Jumu'ah (chapter 62) of the Holy Qur'an was revealed to the Holy Prophet, peace and blessings of Allah be upon him, we happened to be there in his company. When he recited the verse *'wa akhareena minhum lamma yalhaqoo bihim,'* that is, 'those of them who would come later and have not yet joined them.'

(This phrase is a part of a verse mentioning the first advent of the Holy Prophet, peace and blessings of Allah be upon him, followed by a reference to the future events saying that in the latter days also there would be some people who would attain the rank of the earlier followers of the Holy Prophet, peace and blessings of Allah be upon him. Apparently, it speaks of a second advent of the Holy Prophet, peace and blessings of Allah be upon him, in the latter days, because this subclause is governed by the verb used earlier to refer to the first advent of the Holy Prophet, peace and blessings of Allah be upon him)

one of those present asked, 'Who are they? 0 Messenger of Allah!' The Holy Prophet, peace and blessings of Allah be upon him, did not pay attention. The man repeated the question two or three times. At that time Salman the Persian was also sitting among us. The Holy Prophet, peace and blessings of Allah be upon him, turned to him, placed his hand on him and said, 'Even if faith ascended to the Pleiades (completely disappearing from the earth), there would be some from his people (In another version 'one man' is mentioned instead of 'some people') who would restore faith (back) to earth." *(Bukhari)*

عَنْ اَبِىْ هُرَيْرَةَ رضى الله عنه قَالَ قَالَ رَسُوْلُ اللهِ ﷺ ٨٧ ـ
وَالَّذِىْ نَفْسِىْ بِيَدِهِ لَيُوْشِكَنَّ اَنْ يَنْزِلَ فِيْكُمُ ابْنُ مَرْيَمَ حَكَمًا
عَدْلاً فَيَكْسِرُ الصَّلِيْبَ وَيَقْتُلُ الْخِنْزِيرَ وَيَضَعُ الْحَرْبَ
وَيَفِيْضُ الْمَالَ حَتّى لاَيَقْبَلَهُ اَحَدٌ حَتّى تَكُوْنَ السَّجْدَةُ
الْوَاحِدَةُ خَيْرًا مِنَ الدُّنْيَا وَمَا فِيْهَا ثُمَّ يَقُوْلُ اَبُوْ هُرَيْرَةَ وَاقْرَؤُا
اِنْ شِئْتُمْ وَاِنْ مِّنْ اَهْلِ الْكِتَبِ اِلاَّ لَيُؤْمِنَنَّ بِهِ قَبْلَ مَوْتِهِ
وَيَوْمَ الْقِيْمَةِ يَكُوْنُ عَلَيْهِمْ شَهِيْدًا ـ

« بخارى كتاب الانبياء باب نزول عيسى بن مريم »

87. Abu Hurairah, God be pleased with him, relates that the Holy Prophet, peace and blessings of Allah be upon him, said:

"By Him in Whose hands is my life, the son of Mary will soon appear among you. He will administer justice. He will break the cross, kill the swine, abolish war (for the sake of religion, under Divine guidance) distribute wealth, but no one will accept it. In those days one prostration before Allah will be better than the world and what it contains." In his narration Abu Hurairah, God be pleased with him, states:

[Note that this is the opinion of Abu Huraira, God be pleased with him, not the words of the Holy Prophet, peace and blessings of Allah be upon him]

'If you wish you may read the verse,'Wa *immin ahlilkitabi illa layu 'minanna bihee qabla mautihi. Wa yaumalqiyamati yakoonu 'alaihim shaheeda.' (Al Nisa':160)* 'And there is none among the People of the Book but will continue to believe in it before his death: and on the Day of Resurrection, he (Jesus) shall be a witness against them." *(Bukhari)*

٨٨ - اَلَا اِنَّ عِيسَى بْنَ مَرْيَمَ لَيْسَ بَيْنِىْ وَبَيْنَهُ نَبِىٌّ وَلَا رَسُوْلٌ اَلَا اِنَّهُ خَلِيْفَتِىْ فِىْ اُمَّتِىْ مِنْ بَعْدِىْ اَلَا اِنَّهُ يَقْتُلُ الدَّجَّالَ وَيَكْسِرُ الصَّلِيْبَ وَيَضَعُ الْجِزْيَةَ وَتَضَعُ الْحَرْبُ اَوْزَارَهَا اَلَا مَنْ اَدْرَكَهُ فَلْيَقْرَأْ عَلَيْهِ السَّلَامَ ـ

« طبرانى الاوسط والصغير »

88. 'Beware, there will be no prophet or messenger between Jesus, the son of Mary, and me. Remember, he shall be my Caliph after me to my people. Remember, he will kill Anti Christ, break the Cross, abolish the taking of *Jizya* (tax collected from defeated people), as there would no longer be any war. Remember, whoever meets him should convey my greetings to him."

(Tabraani)

٨٩ - عَنْ اَنَسٍ رضى الله عنه قَالَ : قَالَ رَسُولُ اللهِ ﷺ مَنْ اَدْرَكَ مِنْكُمْ عِيسَى ابْنَ مَرْيَمَ فَلْيَقْرَئْهُ مِنِّى السَّلَامَ ـ

« درمنثور ص ٢٤٥/ ج ٢ »

89. Anas, God be pleased with him, states that the Holy Prophet, peace and blessings of Allah be upon him, said:
    Whoever from among you meets Jesus, son of Mary, should convey my greetings to him." *(Durr-e-Manthur)*

٩٠ - عَنْ ثَوْبَانَ قَالَ قَالَ رَسُولُ اللهِ ﷺ فَاِذَا رَئَيْتُمُوهُ فَبَايِعُوْهُ وَلَوْ حَبْوًا عَلَى الثَّلْجِ فَاِنَّهُ خَلِيْفَةُ اللهِ الْمَهْدِى ـ

« ابن ماجه كتاب الفتن »

90. Thaubaan, God be pleased with him, relates that the Holy Prophet, peace and blessings of Allah be upon him, said:

'When you find the Mahdi, perform *bai'ah* (pledge of allegiance) at his hands. You must go to him, even if you have to reach him across icebound mountains on your knees. He is the Mahdi and the Caliph of Allah." *(Ibn Maajah)*

٩١ - عَنْ أَبِى هُرَيْرَةَ رضى الله عنه قَالَ : قَالَ رَسُوْلُ اللهِ ﷺ
كَيْفَ اَنْتُمْ اِذَا نَزَلَ ابْنُ مَرْيَمَ فِيْكُمْ وَاِمَـامُكُمْ مِنْكُمْ وَفِيْ
رِوَايَةٍ فَاَمَّكُمْ مِنْكُمْ .

«بخارى كتاب الانبياء نزول عيسى بن مريم - مسند احمد
ص ٢/٣٣٦ »

91. Abu Hurairah, God be pleased with him, relates that the Holy Prophet, peace and blessings of Allah be upon him, said:

"What a (wretched) state you will be in when the son of Mary will descend among you while he will be your Imam (religious leader) from among you? In another version it is said, 'He will lead you from among you.' *(Bukhari)*

٩٢ - عَنْ مُحَمَّدِ بْنِ عَلِيٍّ رضى الله عنه قَالَ اِنَّ لِمَهْدِيْنَا ايَتَيْنِ لَمْ
تَكُوْنَا مُنْذُ خَلْقِ السَّمْوَاتِ وَالاَرْضِ يَنْكَسِفُ الْقَمَرُ لاِوَّلِ
لَيْلَةٍ مِنْ رَمَضَانَ وَيَنْكَسِفُ الشَّمْسُ فِى النِّصْفِ مِنْهُ وَلَمْ
تَكُوْنَا مُنْذُ خَلَقَ اللَّهُ السَّمْوٰتِ وَالاَرْضَ .

«سنن دارقطنى باب صفة صلوة الخسوف والكسوف
وهيئتها »

92. Muhammad bin Ali, God be pleased with him, said:

"Surely two signs will appear for our Mahdi which have never appeared before (as signs of truth for anyone else), since the creation of heaven and earth. In the month of Ramadhan, the moon will be eclipsed on the first of its nights (of eclipse),* and the sun will be eclipsed on the middle day (of its days of eclipse). Both these eclipses will take place in the same month of Ramadhan. And these two signs have never occured before since Allah created the heavens and the earth." *(Sunan Dar Qutni)*

*[obviously the first night of the month is not meant here, because the moon is not referred to as 'hilal' (crescent) the word applicable to the first three days of the moon's appearance. Moreover, the moon of the first night can never be eclipsed, not to mention the difficulty of sighting it]

٩٣ - عَنْ سُلَيْمَانَ بْنِ عَمْرِو بْنِ الأَحْوَصِ قَالَ حَدَّثَنِيْ أَبِيْ أَنَّهُ شَهِدَ حَجَّةَ الْوَدَاعِ مَعَ رَسُولِ اللهِ ﷺ فَحَمِدَ اللهَ وَأَثْنَى عَلَيْهِ وَذَكَرَ وَوَعَظَ ثُمَّ قَالَ: أَيُّ يَوْمٍ أَحْرَمُ أَيُّ يَوْمٍ أَحْرَمُ ، أَيُّ يَوْمٍ أَحْرَمُ ؟ قَالَ فَقَالَ النَّاسُ: يَوْمُ الْحَجِّ الأَكْبَرِ يَارَسُولَ اللهِ . قَالَ: فَإِنَّ دِمَائَكُمْ وَأَمْوَالَكُمْ وَأَعْرَاضَكُمْ عَلَيْكُمْ حَرَامٌ كَحُرْمَةِ يَوْمِكُمْ هٰذَا ، فِىْ بَلَدِكُمْ هٰذَا ، فِىْ شَهْرِكُمْ هٰذَا ، أَلاَ لاَيَجْنِىْ جَانٍ إِلاَّ عَلَى نَفْسِهِ ، وَلاَ يَجْنِىْ وَالِدٌ عَلَى وَلَدِهِ ، وَلاَ وَلَدٌ عَلَى وَالِدِهِ ، أَلاَ إِنَّ الْمُسْلِمَ أَخُو الْمُسْلِمِ ، فَلَيْسَ يَحِلُّ لِمُسْلِمٍ مِنْ أَخِيْهِ شَىْءٌ إِلاَّ مَا أَحَلَّ مِنْ نَفْسِهِ ، أَلاَ وَإِنَّ كُلَّ رِبَاٍ فِى الْجَاهِلِيَّةِ مَوْضُوعٌ ، لَكُمْ رُؤُسُ أَمْوَالِكُمْ لاَتَظْلِمُونَ وَلاَ تُظْلَمُونَ غَيْرَ رِبَا الْعَبَّاسِ بْنِ عَبْدِ الْمُطَّلِبِ فَإِنَّهُ مَوْضُوعٌ كُلُّهُ ، أَلاَ وَإِنَّ كُلَّ دَمٍ كَانَ فِى الْجَاهِلِيَّةِ مَوْضُوعٌ ، وَأَوَّلُ دَمٍ أَضَعُ مِنْ دَمِ الْجَاهِلِيَّةِ دَمَ الْحَارِثِ ابْنِ عَبْدِالْمُطَّلِبِ ، كَانَ مُسْتَرْضَعًا فِىْ بَنِىْ لَيْثٍ فَقَتَلَتْهُ هُذَيْلٌ . أَلاَ وَاسْتَوْصُوا بِالنِّسَاءِ خَيْراً ، فَإِنَّمَاهُنَّ عَوَانٌ عِنْدَكُمْ ، لَيْسَ تَمْلِكُونَ مِنْهُنَّ شَيْئًا غَيْرَ ذٰلِكَ

إلَّا أَنْ يَأْتِينَ بِفَاحِشَةٍ مُبَيِّنَةٍ ، فَإِنْ فَعَلْنَ فَاهْجُرُوهُنَّ فِى الْمَضَاجِعِ وَاضْرِبُوهُنَّ ضَرْبًا غَيْرَ مُبَرِّحٍ ، فَإِنْ أَطَعْنَكُمْ فَلَاتَبْغُوا عَلَيْهِنَّ سَبِيلًا ـ أَلَا وَإِنَّ لَكُمْ عَلَى نِسَائِكُمْ حَقًّا وَلِنِسَائِكُمْ عَلَيْكُمْ حَقًّا ، فَأَمَّا حَقُّكُمْ عَلَى نِسَائِكُمْ فَلَا يُوطِئْنَ فُرُشَكُمْ مَنْ تَكْرَهُونَ ، وَلَايَأْذَنَّ فِى بُيُوتِكُمْ لِمَنْ تَكْرَهُونَ أَلَا وَإِنَّ حَقَّهُنَّ عَلَيْكُمْ أَنْ تُحْسِنُوا إِلَيْهِنَّ فِى كِسْوَتِهِنَّ وَطَعَامِهِنَّ ـ

« ترمذى أبواب التفسير سورة التوبه »

93. Sulaiman bin 'Amr bin Al Ahwas,God be pleased with him, relates that his father told him that he had witnessed the Last Pilgrimage of the Holy Prophet, peace and blessings of Allah be upon him,:

"The Holy Prophet, peace and blessings of Allah be upon him, praised Allah and glorified Him and admonished the assembly, and asked: 'Which is the most sacred day? Which is the most sacred day? Which is the most sacred day?' The people replied: 'The day of the greatest hajj, 0 Messenger of Allah.' The Prophet said: 'Remember then that your lives, your belongings, and your honour have the same sanctity as this day, this city, and this month. No one will be held accountable except for his own deeds. A father will not be accountable for the deeds of his son. A son will not be held accountable for the deeds of his father. Remember that every Muslim is a brother to a Muslim. No one should appropriate anything belonging to his brother, except with his permission. Remember that all interest on loans made in the Days of ignorance is abolished, except for the capital, which remains yours. Do not wrong anyone and you will not be wronged. So also the interest due to 'Abbas bin Abdul Muttalib [a close relative of the Holy Prophet, peace and blessings of Allah be upon him,] is abolished entirely. All blood that has been shed in the pagan period is to be left unavenged. The first claim on blood I abolish is that of Ibn Rabi 'a bin Al Harith bin 'Abdul Muttalib [a close relative of his] who was fostered among the Banu Layth and whom Hudhayl killed. Admonish each other to treat women with kindness for they are your trusts (You will be accountable for them). You have no authority over them except if they are guilty of glaring misconduct. If they are, then leave them alone in their beds and chastise them, but not too severly. If they obey, you have no justification (to be harsh to them), so seek none. Remember you have certain rights over your women; so also have your women certain rights over you.Your right over them is that they should lead chaste lives. They should not allow any person in your home of whom you disapprove. Their right over you is that you are made responsible for their livelihood."   *(Tirmidhi)*